THE ASSERTIVE SOC

The Assertive Social Worker

Patricia McBride

© Patricia McBride 1998

Published by
Arena
Ashgate Publishing Limited
Gower House
Croft Road
Aldershot
Hants GU11 3HR
England

Ashgate Publishing Company
Old Post Road
Brookfield
Vermont 05036
USA

British Library Cataloguing in Publication Data
McBride, Patricia
 The assertive social worker
 1. Social workers – Psychology 2. Assertiveness training
 I. Title
 361.3

Library of Congress Cataloging-in-Publication Data

McBride, Patricia, 1946–   .
  The assertive social worker : Patricia McBride.
    p.   cm.
  Includes bibliographical references and index.
  ISBN 1-85742-421-2 (pbk.)
  1. Social workers—Psychology. 2. Social workers—Attitudes.
 3. Social workers–In-service training.
 4. Assertiveness (Psychology) 5. Assertiveness training. I. Title.
 HV40.M445   1998
 361.3'2'019–dc21
                                                              97-44525
                                                              CIP

ISBN: 1 85742 421 2

Typeset in Palatino by Raven Typesetters, Chester and printed in Great Britain by Biddles Ltd, Guildford and King's Lynn.

Contents

List of figures and tables   vii

Introduction   ix

1   Understanding assertive behaviour   1

2   Barriers to assertiveness and how to overcome them   17

3   Looking the part: Non-verbal communication   35

4   Establishing rapport   45

5   Your rights as a social worker and as an individual   57

6   Making requests   71

7   Attending and chairing meetings   81

8   Giving feedback   91

9   Learning from criticism   103

10   Saying 'No' and setting boundaries   117

11   Handling aggression   125

12   Negotiation skills   141

13   Handling passivity in others   159

14   Keeping calm and confidence-building   167

Postscript   179

Bibliography   181

Index   183

List of figures and tables

Figures
1.1   Behaviour styles   5
3.1   Verbal versus non-verbal communication   35
4.1   Eye movement and representational systems   54
5.1   Rights and beliefs cycle   59
9.1   The Johari Window   104
9.2   Bad attention – Rebellious Child   106
9.3   Accepting all criticism – Adapted Child   106

Tables
1.1   Four styles of behaviour   13
2.1   Ego states and communication style   24
2.2   Games and how to counter them   29
2.3   A social worker's game   31
3.1   Non-verbal aspects of behaviour   36
4.1   Specifying goals   46
5.1   Assertive rights as an individual   58
5.2   Workers' rights   62
5.3   Managers' rights   65
6.1   Sarah's list   74
8.1   Reasons we shouldn't criticise others   92
8.2   Being specific   94
8.3   Criticising the behaviour, not the person   96
8.4   Errol's four-step approach   98
9.1   Ego state responses to criticism   107
9.2   Responding to sarcasm   113
11.1 Dealing with confrontation   135
13.1 Different types of passivity (non-assertion)   160

Introduction

Would you like to feel more in control of yourself and your work? Cope comfortably with any demands the day throws at you? Deal easily with situations without guilt or worry?

All of these things are possible because you can control your behaviour.

If you're not in control of your mind, who is?

People sometimes worry that becoming assertive will change their basic personality, make them someone that others won't want to know. In fact, when people become truly assertive (as opposed to aggressive) the opposite happens. People like being around assertive people because they are open, honest and respectful of others whilst also looking after their own needs.

Another worry sometimes expressed is that learning to be assertive is too difficult because of well-established behaviour patterns stemming from childhood. This is a realistic concern. We all behave in the way we do today because at some previous time in our life such behaviour has served us well. Perhaps we fear speaking up against the majority because in our family of origin this brought condemnation or mockery. Perhaps we react aggressively to situations because that was the only way to get heard as a child. Perhaps we are sarcastic to others because as a child this helped us to retaliate without tears.

So we should never blame ourselves for behaving in a way that was once appropriate – as children, we do what we can to get love. However, as adults, such behaviours may no longer be appropriate. Now, as social workers and probation officers, we must be able to speak up for ourselves and clients. We must be able to keep calm when provoked. We must be able to negotiate in an adult way.

Overcoming early conditioning is, of course, difficult. You could go into years of therapy to increase your confidence and communication skills. But there's another way: learn to be assertive. Treat these new ways of behaving as simply a skill. You have learned many new skills in your life, and what once seemed difficult is now everyday – driving is a good example. By treating assertiveness as a set of skills you can improve your communication and your self-esteem. Because by behaving more assertively you will feel happier about yourself. You'll feel in control of yourself and any situation. Not only that, people will respond to you differently, with more respect, and that in itself will increase your self-esteem.

Remember, being assertive is a skill like any other – you can learn new techniques and improve your ability with practice. But, like any new skills, the first steps can feel daunting. Let's use learning to drive as an analogy for the steps to learning:

- **Step 1: Unconsciously incompetent** – Before we start learning to drive we don't go around all day thinking, 'Oh dear, I don't know how to do a three point turn!' We just go about our daily business completely incompetent in terms of driving skills.
- **Step 2: Consciously incompetent** – Now we start driving lessons. Suddenly it is painfully clear what we don't know. The driving instructor tells us to turn left at the top of the hill. Panic! So many things to remember. Will we ever learn to indicate, look in the mirror, check over our shoulder and change gear all at once? This is a very uncomfortable stage in the learning process.
- **Step 3: Consciously competent** – We're getting the hang of this driving business now. The driving instructor tells us to turn left at the top of the hill and we calmly talk ourselves through the process, 'Indicate, look in the mirror, check over shoulder, change gear.' We can do it but we still have to think about it.
- **Step 4: Unconsciously competent** – We arrive at work completely unaware of the journey, our thoughts having been miles away.

The same process will be true when you learn and begin using assertion skills. You will become much more aware of your own behaviour, as well as that of others. You'll be more reflective of how you handled situations. Sometimes you'll crunch the gears, other times you'll negotiate a tricky corner smoothly and effortlessly. All perfectly normal in the process of learning.

So don't be hard on yourself. If you oversteer and behave in the opposite manner to that intended, just learn from the experience. If you avoid that skid with ease, reflect on the skills used so that you can repeat them.

Treat this book as a journey, a revisiting of your old and well-trusted communication skills and a trip to some new ones to help guide you through every aspect of your life. Being assertive is exhilarating, it can turn your whole life around. Relax, trust yourself and enjoy the journey. Good luck in your social work or probation career.

1 Understanding assertive behaviour

Social work is a stimulating and exciting job. It is also a frustrating and exhausting one – so many demands on your time, so much knowledge to carry in your head, so many different personality types to deal with. Indeed, it is easy to get so caught up in the challenges of the work that it becomes difficult to see the wood for the trees. When this happens we can fail to step back and look at our communication style and how it affects our interaction with others. We can also overlook how our style may affect our stress level.

Let's look at typical situations in which assertive communication skills and a calm approach are needed by social workers:

- a case review where your views differ from the majority of the meeting
- being questioned in court by an aggressive barrister
- a client suddenly shouting and shaking a fist at you
- a colleague failing to undertake their share of the work
- a boss giving inadequate supervision
- an elderly, confused person smearing faeces for the third time in a day

These and many other difficult situations are the everyday lot of the social worker. Whether it's face-to-face work with clients, telephone communication or dealing with colleagues, there is always a challenge around the corner.

So how do you score at present in your assertion skills? Here is a simple questionnaire to help you assess your current state. For each question select one answer that is most true for you and mark it with a tick. Answer quickly and without pondering on each question at length. If none of the responses feels quite right for you, go for the one nearest to what you would do.

Assessing your current assertion skills

1   You are visiting the mother of three young children. You suspect she is a heavy drinker. You ask her how much she has drunk in the previous 24 hours. 'Nothing,' she replies, although you can smell alcohol on her breath. Do you say:

    a   .... Nothing.
    b   .... 'I've smelt alcohol on your breath, do you think I'm a fool?'
    c   .... 'I've smelt alcohol on your breath. I'm concerned about you. How much have you had to drink today?'
    d   .... 'Oh yes, and that's tea fumes you're breathing at me, is it?'

2   You have a great deal of work on. Your boss asks you to take on another case which you suspect will involve a lot of work. Do you:

    a   .... Agree to take the case.
    b   .... Sigh heavily and say 'Of course, I've got nothing else to do, have I?'
    c   .... Shout 'You must be joking!' and leave the room.
    d   .... Say 'You know I'd help if I could, but I'm too busy at the moment.'

3   You are giving a client a lift to the Benefit Office. The client takes a cigarette packet from their pocket. You don't like anyone smoking in your car. Do you:

    a   .... Slam on the brakes and say 'You know I don't agree with smoking. Find your own damn way to the Benefit Office.'
    b   .... Say 'Well, we've all got to die of something, haven't we?'
    c   .... Cough gently and open the window but say nothing.
    d   .... Say 'I'm sorry, but I don't allow smoking in my car.'

4   A GP makes a racist comment. Do you:

    a   .... Say 'I find that remark offensive.'
    b   .... Say 'Mmm.'
    c   .... Sigh heavily and say 'Well, of course you would say that, wouldn't you.'
    d   .... Say sharply 'I hate working with racist people.'

5   A client makes a rude remark about one of your colleagues. Do you:

    a   .... Quietly say 'You may be right.'
    b   .... Say 'How dare you say that after all she did for you!'
    c   .... Say 'And I suppose you're perfect, are you?'
    d   .... Say 'That's not my experience.'

6   You are in the witness stand. A barrister aggressively asks you the same question for the third time. Do you:

    a   .... Glare and refuse to answer.

b .... Say 'How many more times do you want me to say the same thing?'
c .... Say 'I feel I have nothing further to add to my previous answers.'
d .... Feel flustered and stutter your answer again.

7 You are chairing a meeting. Two of the participants begin to argue about an issue. Do you:

a .... Shout over them, telling them to cool it.
b .... Look helplessly at the others in the meeting.
c .... Call 'Children, Children!'
d .... Stand up and say 'I'd like us to find some common ground here. Can we calm down and look at the matter again?'

8 You are at an elderly client's house where you have called together a meeting of several professionals you have co-ordinated to help the client. The client says loudly and sulkily, 'You social workers are all the bloody same. Waste of time, you don't get anything done.' Do you:

a .... Refuse to be drawn, and continue the meeting to resolve the person's needs.
b .... Say 'You ungrateful old . . .'
c .... Say quietly 'I wish there was more I could do.'
d .... Say 'What do you think all these people are doing here then?'

9 You are a probation officer and you have to write a report at short notice for the court. Your client has failed to keep three appointments. You bump into him/her in the town centre. Do you:

a .... Smile and make another appointment, saying nothing about the missed ones.
b .... Say sharply 'Where the hell have you been?'
c .... Ask if they've forgotten their way to your office.
d .... Say that if they don't keep the next appointment you will notify the court.

10 A planning meeting is almost finished when your boss suddenly suggests something that goes against all previous agreements reached. No one else says anything. Do you:

a .... Sigh loudly and mutter just loud enough for others to hear 'Oh yes, and I suppose I'll be the one to pick up the pieces.'
b .... Keep quiet – after all, no one else is objecting.
c .... Say loudly 'You must be joking. Haven't you heard anything that's been said so far?'
d .... Say 'I can't agree with that course of action. How do other people feel?'

Scoring

To score your questionnaire, circle on the score sheet below your answer to each of the ten questions. When you have done this, add your scores vertically.

Question	Assertive	Aggressive	Passive	Indirectly aggressive
1	c	d	a	b
2	d	c	a	b
3	d	a	c	b
4	a	d	b	c
5	d	b	a	c
6	c	b	d	a
7	d	a	b	c
8	a	b	c	d
9	d	b	a	c
10	d	c	b	a
Totals				

How did you get on? Obviously the more 'assertive' replies you scored the better. Do you see a clear picture emerging of yourself as an assertive, passive, aggressive or indirectly aggressive person? Perhaps you realise that you are assertive in some situations but not in others. It is very common for people to be assertive in one area of their lives but aggressive or passive at other times. Likewise, people often say they are assertive with some people but not others. For example, many people report that they find it difficult to be assertive with older or more senior people.

This type of questionnaire also highlights the fact that not only *what* you say but *how* you say it affects the message you give others. In some cases, the same words can be said assertively, aggressively, passively or indirectly aggressively. What changes the message is your tone of voice and body language. These will be discussed further in Chapter 3.

Four behaviour styles

To help understand assertive behaviour more thoroughly it is helpful to compare it with other behaviours. A useful approach is to look at four styles of behaviour and how they differ from each other (see Figure 1.1).

Assertive Behaviour	Aggressive Behaviour
'I'm OK, you're OK' (underlying belief about self is that they *are* OK)	*'I'm OK, you're not OK'* (underlying belief about self is that they are *not* OK)
Passive Behaviour	**Indirectly Aggressive Behaviour**
'I'm not OK, you're OK' (underlying belief about self is that they are *not* OK)	*'I'm OK, you're not OK, but I won't tell you I think that'* (underlying belief about self is that they are *not* OK)

Figure 1.1   Behaviour styles

The assertive social worker

There are many popular misconceptions about what assertive behaviour actually is. It's one of those words like 'gay' and 'green' that have changed their meaning over the years. 'Assertive' used to mean being aggressive, a bully, disrespecting others. Now it means something quite different.

Being assertive means:

- having appropriate behaviour that is halfway between aggressive and passive
- feeling confident about yourself
- respecting yourself and others equally
- having clear goals and outcomes
- being able to say that you don't know or don't understand
- speaking out for yourself or others
- making your opinion heard in a way that doesn't harm others
- listening to others' points of view even if you don't agree
- not putting others down

- having confident and appropriate body language
- choosing behaviour most appropriate to the situation

Being assertive is *not:*

- bullying others
- failing to hear what others are saying
- treating others without respect
- wimping out of difficult situations
- getting your own way at all costs
- looking submissive
- always responding to situations in the same way

The basis of assertion is respect for yourself and others: a belief that 'I'm OK and you're OK.' Developing this equal respect is not easy. 'Parent messages' (explored in more detail in Chapter 2) tell the growing child about their position in life, their value and what to think about others, so if you have poor self-esteem you will find it difficult to treat others equally because you'll have underlying feelings that they're more important than you. Likewise, if you have any prejudices, you are likely to treat people with less respect than they deserve.

Social workers and those in the helping professions should be well aware of the need to treat people without discrimination. However, even if we have no obvious prejudices, like race or gender, driving our behaviour, we can treat people with disrespect simply because we dislike them or what they do. The assertive social worker acknowledges openly that certain behaviours are completely unacceptable. But treating the client without respect because of what they have done is certain to raise barriers to effective communication.

Respect is the key to achieving a win–win situation, something the assertive social worker sets out to reach. Whilst acknowledging that it is impossible for everyone to come away from every communication having achieved exactly what they want, the assertive social worker aims to leave everyone feeling that the best possible outcome has been accomplished.

Assertive social workers reach workable compromises but don't compromise themselves.

To do this the social worker must be clear about goals and outcomes. Each communication should have a purpose identified before the meeting and unambiguously conveyed to the client or colleague. However, assertiveness is also about listening to others and being flexible where appropriate. Sometimes no flexibility is possible – the client *must* change certain behaviours to avoid a child being taken into care or being referred back to the court. Other outcomes may have a more flexible route and sometimes the client may suggest alternative and achievable ways to reach a goal. This may mean working out an acceptable compromise with both parties.

The assertive social worker:

- **is clear about outcomes to be achieved** and conveys them unambiguously to others – 'This term you must collect your child promptly from school every day.'
- **makes his or her feelings known,** and does this in a respectful way – 'I'm unhappy about the way you handled that situation.'
- **lets others know his or her boundaries** so that they are clear about what can and cannot be achieved – 'I can help with contacting the Housing Department, but I can't promise a result.'
- **strives for a win–win situation** to leave everyone feeling as satisfied as possible – 'This seems to be the best solution for everyone.'
- **will reach a workable compromise** but will not compromise own integrity – 'I will contact the Benefits Agency for you if you start writing down your outgoings.'
- **says 'No' clearly and without guilt** to avoid misunderstandings and wasted time and energy – 'I'm sorry, I can't give you extra community care time.'
- **gives appropriate praise** to motivate others – 'I'm really pleased with the way you handled your money this week.'
- **gives criticism constructively** to help the other person, not as a payoff – 'I cannot accept what you said about your child.'
- **learns from criticism** and decides whether to change their behaviour as a result – 'Thank you for telling me that.'
- **can express anger constructively** without having to actually lose his or her temper – 'I'm very angry that you behaved that way.'

Above all, being assertive is about having the widest possible range of behaviour options available. Strange though it may seem, this means that you may actually *choose* to be aggressive or passive at times. For example, you may have tried all possible assertive methods with a client, but now you realise that when you are angry they are more likely to respond. Alternatively, you may agree to cover duty for a colleague even though it is inconvenient for you because you know they are particularly hard pushed at the time.

The difference is that by making the *choice* of behaviour you are still really being assertive. To wimp out or lose your temper is not making a choice. Selecting your behaviour *is*.

The person with the widest range of behaviour options is likely to be the most successful in any communication.

So how can you tell if you've made a choice or are simply kidding yourself? Listen to your body – it will tell you. If you've simply lost control, you'll feel bad, cringe or kick yourself. If you've truly made a choice, you'll feel quite comfortable with yourself.

Exercise

Think of a time when you have been assertive.

- What made it possible for you to be assertive?
- What skills did you use?
- Who were you communicating with?
- How did you feel immediately before the incident?
- How did you feel during and after the incident?
- What can you learn from this previous experience that you can use for the future?

The aggressive social worker

Unlike the assertive person, whose underlying message is 'I respect you. You're OK and I'm OK,' the aggressive social worker's message is 'I don't respect you. I'm OK and you're not OK.' However, this is unlikely to reflect the aggressive person's real feelings about themself. People who truly feel OK about themselves find little need to be aggressive on a regular basis.

Aggression usually covers up some feeling of inadequacy. Perhaps the social worker learned early in life that this is the only way to get listened to. Perhaps the aggression is a result of inappropriately expressed frustration.

The aggressive social worker:

- **puts his or her own needs before others**
- **fails to listen well**
- **does not respect other people**
- **antagonises others**
- **blames others**
- **ignores the rights of others**
- **refuses to take responsibility for mistakes**
- **does not consider all viewpoints**

Aggression is more typically a male behaviour in British society, but by no means exclusively so. However, aggressive women are likely to be seen as more extreme than men exhibiting the same behaviour, because of the expectation that women should be mild and obliging at all times.

In the short term aggression may have some advantages. Aggressive people often get their own way, particularly if they are in a position of authority, such as a social worker or manager. People will back off and give in because they would rather avoid confrontation. Aggressive people are able to kid themselves that they are perfect, refusing to look at their own painful failings.

But in the long term aggressive behaviour is destructive and unhelpful. People avoid those who are aggressive because they don't much like them. And social workers who are aggressive get a variety of negative responses from clients. Clients may be too nervous to tell them that things aren't going to plan; the social worker will only find out when things have gone very wrong. Other clients may give an aggressive response, possibly even putting the social worker at physical risk. And people often sabotage those who are aggressive: colleagues don't co-operate with swapping duty, clients fail to keep appointments, admin staff 'forget' to pass on messages.

Case study – Edith

Edith, a 51-year-old social worker with ten years' experience, was well known as the office bully. She always found the least confident (usually the newest) person in the office to pick on. As they developed more confidence, she found someone else to bully. Her verbal bullying was often subtle and accompanied with a smile, but the underlying message of disregard was always there. Edith wondered why she had few friends and others refused to co-work on cases with her. She was never offered promotion.

The passive social worker

The passive social worker's underlying message is 'You're more important than me. You can ignore my needs – I do.' In effect, 'You're OK, I'm not OK.' And indeed this is the passive person's belief system. Women are more likely to be passive/submissive than men in British society, although there are of course plenty of exceptions. Men who are passive are likely to be judged more harshly than women because of a cultural belief system that they should be tough and strong.

The passive social worker:

- **does not look after their own needs**
- **puts others before themselves**
- **does not stand up for their clients or themselves**
- **avoids conflict at all costs**

- **constantly looks after others**
- **ignores their own rights**
- **often has much unexpressed anger**
- **doesn't ask for what they need**
- **can't say 'No'**
- **won't speak out against the majority in meetings**

The compassion trap

Social work commonly attracts people who 'want to help' and who are compassionate towards others. There is nothing wrong with these sentiments (even though most social workers would not admit to them). However, compassion can mean that in your drive to serve others you fail to look after yourself. In our culture, the compassion trap is common amongst women, many of whom feel that serving others is a way of being recognised legitimately. Such activities are, of course, a rightful choice, but they must be just that – a *choice*. Many social workers are caught up in the compassion trap to such an extent that they don't know how to escape – to make the choice about whether to be compassionate or not. Being in the compassion trap leads to passive behaviour in relation to your own needs.

Passive social workers do not look after their own needs, feeling they have no right to do so. They believe their own rights are less important than those of others.

Social workers who are only slightly passive may be rather popular in the short term. After all, they avoid conflict at all costs. This means that they do anything for anyone even if it is inconvenient. They don't say 'No' to anyone, so they take on too much work, they do everyone's duty, and make tea and coffee endlessly. They often have a ready, if rather nervous, smile. Passive people may be liked, but they are unlikely to be respected. They are even less likely to get promotion. They can be good people to have in the team – in the short term.

In the longer term passive social workers can become rather irritating. At first it may not be obvious that they are passive. Not all passive people are quiet; many are rather talkative. But their colleagues come to learn that they don't look after their own needs, so they often end up looking after them. This places a responsibility on the other person, who ends up at times treating the passive social worker almost as a client. This will be particularly acute in the case of a very passive person. Others constantly have to second guess their wishes to avoid abusing their helpfulness.

Passive social workers have particular difficulties with clients:

- They rarely feel able to say difficult things directly – this can lead to the client receiving mixed messages, if indeed the message is given at all.

- They can easily be manipulated by clients, who quickly learn that the social worker can be persuaded to do anything for them, being unable to say 'No.'
- They may fail to keep clients to task.

Case study – Mary

Mary had a case where two children were on the Child Protection Register because of their mother's lifestyle and inconsistent parenting skills. Sara, the mother, elected not to attend a Child Protection Meeting, and Mary called on her to convey the result of the meeting. It had been decided that Sara had to reach and maintain a range of goals, otherwise at the next meeting consideration would be given to going to court to have the children taken into care. Mary found it very difficult to convey some harsh messages assertively, and told Sara what she had to do in an unclear manner without conveying its importance.

At the next meeting it was decided to go to court because Sara had not met her goals. When Sara learnt this she was furious: 'No one told me it was so important. I didn't realise what I had to do!' Whether or not she would have reached and maintained acceptable standards was in one sense immaterial – Mary had failed her by not being assertive.

Collecting 'stamps'

Because passive people fail to look after their own needs they often become quietly resentful and angry. Eric Berne (1979) refers to the passive person's behaviour in this situation as 'collecting stamps'. Each time you fail to deal with something which annoys you, you put a stamp in a mental savings book. You don't tell the other person that they have irritated you, so they continue with the same behaviour. Common examples would be clients turning up late for appointments or colleagues failing to wash up the coffee mugs.

Eventually, though, even a passive person will lose their temper. They swing directly and swiftly from being passive to being aggressive, shouting at the other person, who is bemused because they had no idea their behaviour was upsetting. The passive person then immediately feels guilty (after all, they *are* a nice person really!) and swings back to being passive, getting out another book ready to collect the next lot of stamps. This is one explanation for why many passive people 'blow up' occasionally.

Of course, stamps are not always collected from the same person. We can collect stamps from different people throughout the day and then go home and kick the cat . . .

The answer is to not collect stamps. Easier said than done, but possible. There are two options. One is to simply throw away the stamp – to decide it's not important and to genuinely not mind. The other is to deal with issues as soon as they begin to irritate – this is a very sound policy. The more stamps in your mental stamp book, the less likely you are to deal with something calmly. But by dealing with something at an early stage, you'll feel calmer, not yet really angry, and much more in control of yourself.

The indirectly aggressive social worker

Aggression comes in many forms. We tend to associate it with shouting and loud voices but it can be much more subtle and sinister. The underlying message of the indirectly aggressive social worker is 'I'm OK, you're not OK – but I won't tell you I think that.' In fact, as with the overtly aggressive social worker, the internal feeling is one of poor self-esteem. There would be no need to score points in this way otherwise.

The indirectly aggressive social worker:

- **is sarcastic**
- **puts down other people**
- **points out others' faults and mistakes even when there is no need to do so**
- **only feels comfortable when they've found flaws in others**
- **criticises indirectly**
- **manipulates others**
- **often denies that offence was intended**

Indirect aggression is just that – indirect. With straightforward aggression you know what you're dealing with – the person is clearly annoyed with you. With indirect aggression you face sarcasm or subtle put-downs which are often denied when challenged. Some examples of this indirect aggression are:

- 'Oh, haven't you sorted that family out yet?'
- 'Have you *still* got her waiting for that grant?'
- 'Mental health work was never your strong point, was it?'
- 'I'm not sure about that report. Did you mean to write it like that or were you in a hurry?'

Table 1.1   Four styles of behaviour

	Assertive	Aggressive	Passive	Indirectly aggressive
Communication style	I will say what I think or feel in a way that respects you and does not damage you.	I am more important than you, I do not respect you. I will say what I want.	I am not important. I will treat you with respect, but you do not have to do the same for me. I will not say what I want.	I am more important than you, but I will not tell you that directly. I will communicate in an unclear way that does not respect your feelings.
Goal	To reach agreement, to communicate clearly	To win at all costs	To avoid confrontation, even if I am inconvenienced	To win without seeming to even be in the competition
In a conflict situation	Keeps calm, objective, looks at all viewpoints	Attacks the other person in order to win	Avoids the conflict	Tries to find someone else to blame

Source: Adapted from Cox & Dainow (1987).

Situational examples

A young mother tells her social worker that she did not attend her child's open day because it coincided with her favourite television programme.

Assertive social worker response: *'I'm sorry to hear that. I'm not sure that's best for Jane. How do you imagine she might be feeling?'*

Passive social worker response: *'Oh, yes it's a good programme isn't it.'*

Aggressive social worker response: *'You're kidding. Have you no idea how Jane feels? Stop thinking about yourself for once.'*

| Indirectly aggressive social worker response: | *'And you really think that's more important than your child's wellbeing, do you? Typical!'* |

A boss cancels supervision yet again. The social worker has several important things to discuss.

Assertive social worker response:	*'I am unhappy that supervision is often cancelled. I need to see you urgently. How quickly can we rearrange our supervision?'*
Aggressive social worker response:	*(loudly) 'Not again! That's the third time you've cancelled supervision in a row. I'm taking this matter higher.'*
Passive social worker response:	*'Oh, OK.'*
Indirectly aggressive social worker response:	*(sighing heavily) 'That's OK then, I'll just carry on regardless, even though I haven't got a clue, shall I?'*

Exercise

Below are three typical social work situations. What would a social worker who is assertive, aggressive, passive or indirectly aggressive say in response to each of the situations?

1   You are on duty with a colleague. S/he went out on a simple visit and didn't return for four hours. This has happened several times before and the person has a reputation for bunking off. You have been very busy as a result of their absence.
2   You are on a joint visit with a colleague when s/he says something to the client which you consider completely unprofessional.
3   For the umpteenth time your line manager arrives fifteen minutes late at a multidisciplinary planning meeting. You feel this makes Social Services look incompetent and unprofessional. Your line manager is constantly late for appointments and you had already asked him/her to be on time for this meeting.

Exercise

Typically people who are not assertive experience guilt, worry, stress and anxiety at times – or even frequently.

Thinking through your current behaviour, try to work out the cost of *not* being assertive. Keep a log for a week of what happened and how you felt during the working day. Then make an action plan for behaviour change. Build in a reward when you have achieved each step. Chapter 14 gives further confidence-building exercises.

Chapter summary

To help us understand assertive behaviour more fully it is useful to look at it in relation to three other behaviours: aggressive behaviour, indirectly aggressive behaviour and passive behaviour (see Figure 1.1).

Assertive behaviour:

- having appropriate behaviour that is halfway between aggressive and passive
- feeling confident about yourself
- respecting yourself and others equally
- having clear goals and outcomes
- being able to say that you don't know or don't understand
- speaking out for yourself or others
- making your opinion heard in a way that doesn't harm others
- listening to others' points of view even if you don't agree
- not putting others down
- having confident and appropriate body language
- choosing behaviour most appropriate to the situation

Aggressive behaviour:

- putting your needs before others
- failing to listen well
- not respecting other people
- antagonising others
- blaming others
- ignoring the rights of others
- refusing to take responsibility for mistakes

● not considering all viewpoints

Passive behaviour:

● not looking after your own needs
● putting others before yourself
● not standing up for your clients or yourself
● avoiding conflict at all costs
● constantly looking after others
● ignoring your own rights
● feeling much unexpressed anger
● not asking for what you need
● being unable to say 'No'
● not speaking out against the majority in meetings

Indirectly aggressive behaviour:

● sarcastic
● putting down other people
● pointing out others' faults and mistakes even when there is no need to do so
● only feeling comfortable when you've found flaws in others
● criticising indirectly
● manipulating others
● often denying that offence was intended

2 Barriers to assertiveness and how to overcome them

Being assertive is about being adult, acting in a commonsense way. All social workers have common sense, don't they? It's the clients who lack it, isn't it?

If only the divide were that clear-cut! If we all employed common sense there would be no social workers who smoked, drank excessively, had sexually transmitted diseases, were overweight, or unfit.

So why do social workers as well as clients sabotage themselves in this way?

In terms of assertive communication one simple answer is that as children we have little practice at it. We are not taught the basic skills and often have poor role models in the adults around us. Indeed, as children many of us were taught to be seen and not heard. We were not allowed to say 'No' to adults without fear of reprisal. We were not taught how to give criticism constructively (and most adults would certainly not welcome it from a child). We were rarely allowed to respond confidently to criticism from adults. Our learning in this area was probably pretty poor.

Gender role models

Our learning in terms of gender, however, is pretty acute. Detailed research has shown that from birth we are handled differently according to our gender. Baby girls are more likely to be cuddled and told how pretty they are, baby boys are more likely to be bounced around and told how strong they are. Although things are changing, the role models we see still tell us clearly how we are expected to behave as males and females. Let's look at a few examples:

- Children's advertising still tends to show little girls playing nicely with dolls whilst little boys zap around with action toys.

17

- Children's books, whilst improving considerably, still tend to show mother in the caring role whilst father is active. And there are still plenty of older traditional books around.
- Drama in film or on television still mostly shows men being more active than women – until *Alien* women were only in space to be rescued! Likewise men rarely cry or express deep, painful emotions (except via anger).
- Sport portrays men being active. Women's sport is very rarely reported in the media.
- Government – the majority of MPs are still male.
- News – anchor newsreaders and experts called upon to explain situations are more often men. War scenes show more men being violent.

So the overall picture is of active men and less active women, despite recent shifts. All of these gender models push females and males into roles they may or may not feel happy with.

Females still find it more difficult to say 'No', assert themselves in meetings, stand up for themselves, put across a point strongly, or attend to their own needs. Males still find it more difficult to show strong emotions other than anger, allow others to look after them, admit when they don't know something, or ask for help. Females are still more likely to show frustration by crying, men by shouting.

Cultural expectations towards gender mean that should a woman and a man both behave in exactly the same assertive way, the woman is likely to be perceived as more aggressive than the man. Women shouldn't worry about this – practise with your style until you are happy it suits the unique person you are.

Parent messages

As children we are learning about ourselves and our world at a phenomenal rate. We receive constant 'parent messages' from significant people in our lives, and these messages tell us about ourselves and the world around us. They come not just from our primary caregivers (although they will naturally have the most influence) but also from teachers, siblings and anyone else with whom we have contact.

Because parent messages are transmitted to us at a stage when our personalities are forming, they are very powerful. Gradually they shape our whole belief system. They tell us what is good, what is bad, what type of person we are, what type of place the world is, everything. Consciously or unconsciously they drive our behaviour – in some cases for the rest of our lives.

Exercise

To get some idea of whether typical parent messages may be driving your behaviour, look at the following messages that are often given to children. Do you recognise any of them as having been given to you (verbally or non-verbally) and if so, how do you think this affects your present-day behaviour?

- 'You'll never amount to anything.'
- 'You're so clumsy.'
- 'You're gorgeous.'
- 'Don't tell anyone.'
- 'We keep our problems to ourselves in this house.'
- 'Always wipe your feet before you come into the house.'
- 'Don't you dare say no to me!'
- 'You're stupid.'
- 'You're the clever one.'
- 'You're ugly.'
- 'You're pretty.'
- 'You can do anything you want if you put your mind to it.'
- 'Children should be seen and not heard.'
- 'Can't you even do that?'
- 'You're such a good girl.'
- 'Stop behaving like a tomboy.'
- 'Boys don't play with dolls.'

Our present behaviour served us well at some previous time. Of course, there may be some behaviours about which we are unhappy. 'I wish I could stop smoking, I know it's bad for me.' 'If I could lose some weight I'd feel so much better about myself.' 'I know I shouldn't have lost my temper during super-vision.' The truth is that at some earlier stage in life the undesired behaviour was effective. Perhaps it was effective to:

- keep quiet in discussions to avoid incurring your parents' wrath
- comfort yourself with food when love was unavailable
- talk loudly because that's the only way you could be heard in your family
- look away when you were angry because as a child it avoided someone saying 'Don't look at me like that!'
- stare at someone because your parents drummed into you 'Look at me when I'm speaking to you!'
- be sweet and helpful to everyone, even at your own expense, because that's what got you the reward of 'That's a good girl.'

- be tough and strong because that was what was admired
- never argue with your parents because otherwise love was withdrawn
- look after everyone because no one else did
- be aggressive because otherwise you never got anything

And so it became necessary to develop defences against hurt. These defences have served a useful purpose – they have kept some harsh reality about ourselves and our situation at bay. Although these defences are a form of self-deception, they should not be mocked – they may be useful. We all have such defences – think of them as hiding places for bits of our innermost self we'd rather keep hidden, often from ourselves as well as from others. However, once we recognise that we have a behaviour we'd like to change, it's helpful to look at our defences to see why we've built them up.

You may or may not be able to recognise the origins of your unwanted behaviour. It's helpful, but if you can't it doesn't really matter. Once you've identified the unwanted behaviour, you can begin to change it. Later in this chapter we'll look at how to overcome limiting beliefs. The remainder of the book will provide you with specific skills to use with your new belief systems to make you a truly assertive social worker.

Developing belief systems about ourselves

Parent messages are both verbal and non-verbal. Let's look first at non-verbal messages. In relation to ourselves as people these would include:

- a smile when we do something well
- a frown when someone is displeased with us
- a slap in anger
- being ignored (withdrawal of love)

Non-verbal messages are very powerful. They are also more frequent than verbal messages because so much of our communication is unspoken. And if verbal and non-verbal messages aren't congruent, the non-verbal will be believed. A parent who says 'I love you, darling' without taking their eyes from the television is actually giving the opposite message. Children don't have to be told they are loved or unloved to understand which is the case.

Turning to verbal messages, children receive these all day every day:

- 'What a good boy.'
- 'What a pretty girl.'
- 'I'm so pleased with his school report.'
- 'The teacher says she's disruptive.'
- 'You're lovely.'

- 'You're hopeless.'
- 'Get out of my sight.'

These messages include not only what is said directly *to* the child but also what is said *about* him or her within earshot.

Praise and criticism are of crucial importance. Criticism is an unavoidable everyday event for a child, but the way in which the criticism is given is vitally important for the developing child's self-esteem. Children who are criticised as a whole person for wrongdoings will have poorer self-esteem than those who are criticised for their actions alone:

Whole-person criticising	Behaviour-only criticising
'You're stupid, you'll never amount to anything.'	'Your maths results were poor.'
	'Your bedroom's a mess.'
'You're a slob.'	'You were careless with that glass.'
'You're clumsy.'	'Wait until I've finished speaking.'
'You've got a big mouth.'	

Being criticised as a whole person tells the child that s/he is of little or no worth. The message can remain embedded for a lifetime. People develop whole belief systems about themselves which have little basis in reality beyond their own limiting beliefs:

- 'I'm not the sort of person who takes risks.'
- 'I can't say difficult things to people.'
- 'I'm no good at maths.'
- 'I can't do that because I'm short/tall/Catholic/Muslim/fat/white/ black', etc.
- 'I can't say "No." '
- 'I'm just a housewife.'
- 'I'm no good in meetings.'
- 'I can't control my temper.'

The whole tenor is that these things are outside the person's control. They're not. The reality is that people can do most things if they are prepared to spend time learning how to do so.

Learning about our world

Other messages tell the child about the world in which they live. They too can be verbal or non-verbal. Verbal messages might include:

- 'We keep our business to ourselves in this family.'

- 'You can't trust men.'
- 'Respect your elders and betters.'
- 'Mutton dressed as lamb.'
- 'Don't ask for anything when you visit your friend.'
- 'Women do nothing but gossip.'
- 'Expect the best but prepare for the worst.'
- 'Don't worry, it'll be all right in the end.'
- 'It's a tough world out there.'
- 'People are kind.'
- 'Things always have a way of sorting themselves out.'
- 'It'll all be the same in 100 years.'

Examples of non-verbal messages about the world might include:

- tidying up before people come to visit
- putting on your best clothes before visiting the doctor
- having daddy's dinner ready before he comes home
- giving the boys the biggest portions of food
- buying different toys for girls and boys
- avoiding people of a different race or colour

Exercise

If you have many negative thoughts about yourself and your behaviour, you are almost certainly failing to appreciate those things that you do well. Below is a checklist to prompt you. Tick the activities you do well. You don't have to be an expert at them – 'good enough' warrants a tick. Fill in the empty spaces at the bottom with any other areas of knowledge or expertise you have.

• listening skills	• counselling skills
• dealing with difficult clients	• coping with emergencies
• comforting distressed people	• being a good colleague
• report writing	• giving evidence in court
• dealing with confused elderly people	• entering the client's world
• keeping focused in your work	• asking for help appropriately

● having your say in meetings	● keeping a balanced view
● maintaining a positive emotional state	● managing your time
● managing your stress level	● knowledge of legislation
●	●
●	●
●	●
●	●

Personality and behaviour

Parent messages and defence systems about which we are unconscious will continue to drive our behaviour. They can stop us being a truly assertive social worker able to do the best for ourselves and our client. However, once we begin to analyse our behaviour and bring these messages to conscious awareness, we can begin to change them.

As we've seen, parent messages can be critical or nurturing. One theory which offers a very useful model of understanding behaviour and which incorporates this idea is Transactional Analysis. Eric Berne, who invented this theory, says that our personality is made up of several components (ego states) and that despite the names he has given them, these have nothing to do with our chronological age. Using a Transactional Analysis perspective we can say that we each get our unique personality according to the percentage of each ego state we possess. There are three major ego states. The first is that part which acts like a **Parent** – sets limits, disciplines, guides, criticises, advises, protects, nurtures, keeps traditions. The second is the **Adult** part which works things out by looking at facts, sorts out best alternatives, is assertive. The third is the **Child** part which is fun-loving, energetic, compliant, rebellious, creative, polite, stubborn – in fact a real mixture of child-like behaviours.

These three major ego states subdivide to give us more understanding of our own and others' 'map of the world'. Table 2.1 shows their effects on our communication style.

Table 2.1   Ego states and communication style

Part of the personality	Typical words or phrases	Effect on communication style
Critical Parent – guides and controls, criticises, sets boundaries	'Don't', 'Ought', 'Never', 'Always', 'No one', 'Should', 'Stop that!'	Too much Critical Parent leads to aggressive behaviour which does not respect the other person.
Nurturing Parent – takes care of others, provides love, warmth and a sense of being valued	'Can I help you?', 'Are you all right?', 'That's good', 'Well done', 'How are things going?'	Positive and motivating, but if you have too much Nurturing Parent in your personality you become a 'smother mother'. Social workers who are smother mothers do things for their clients instead of empowering them to do things for themselves. In this way by being 'kind' they actually stop the other person's development.
Adult – assertive, confident, logical, rational, questioning	'How?', 'What?', 'When?', 'Where?', 'Who?', 'How can we . . . ?'	Assertive, confident, logical, rational, goal-centred, calm.
Free Child – likes to have fun, is spontaneous, messes about	'Let's leave this and . . .', 'Whoopee!', 'Coming for a drink?', 'I want . . .'	We should all have fun, but too much of this aspect of the personality and we become rather wearisome for others because there are times when we have to be serious too.
Adapted Child – is adapted to living with others and being polite	'Please', 'Thank you', 'Sorry', 'I didn't mean to . . .', 'Are you really OK?'	Too much of this aspect and we become passive, unable to stand up for ourselves or our clients.

Part of the personality	Typical words or phrases	Effect on communication style
Little Professor – intuitive, just knows when things are going to happen, uses instinct, is curious	'I just knew that would happen', 'How does that work?', 'Wow!'	Curious, energetic, questioning.
Rebellious Child – likes to oppose others in some way	'It wasn't me!', 'I'm just coming' (but doesn't), 'But I'm only half an hour late', 'I forgot', 'It's not fair'	Can be either overtly or covertly rebellious, leading to either overt aggression or indirect aggression.

The Rebellious Child aspect of the personality is worth exploring in more detail. Social workers see a lot of this type of personality (and some Rebellious Children are your colleagues!).

The very worst thing for a child psychologically is to be ignored. The child grows up with no sense of itself, and in extreme cases will fail to thrive even though adequately fed. Children, then, want attention and if they can't get it by being good, they'll settle for getting it by being bad. This means that they grow up being 'rewarded' for bad behaviour.

Take an everyday situation. Jane is talking to her social worker. Young Simon is standing waiting politely to say something. Jane and the social worker continue to talk and Simon is ignored. He gradually becomes bored and misbehaves. Jane gives him some attention (moans at him). She has unintentionally 'rewarded' his bad behaviour.

Negative attention is better than no attention. If this type of negative attention is all the child receives, it grows up unable to 'hear' positive feedback, never having learnt to apply it to itself when younger. Thus you get a Rebellious Child personality. They can come in two forms. One is the outwardly rebellious 'in your face' person – you're in no doubt what's going on with them. The other is much trickier. This is the very nice person who constantly fails to come up with the goods – to do what you know they are well able to do. It is as if they are asking to be told off (which unconsciously is the case). Very confusing – a nice person but a very frustrating one.

If you have a client with a strong Rebellious Child personality the usual motivators to improvement don't work. Positive feedback is not heard. Negative feedback gives them what they unconsciously want. The best option is to give negative feedback and follow it quickly with positive comments and suggestions – and of course, keep assertive at all times.

Behaviour at work questionnaire

The questionnaire below gives a guide to your preferred Parent/Adult/Child ego state at work (i.e. your most common way of behaving). Like any questionnaire it can provide a guide only – we often behave and feel differently depending on the situation and person we are dealing with. However, it provides useful food for thought.

Indicate how often you exhibit each of the following behaviours by placing a tick in the column opposite each item, e.g. if you frequently feel uncomfortable for ages about something you've said to a colleague or they've said to you, put a tick in the box under 'frequently'.

Behaviour at work	Frequency				
	Almost never	Rarely	Sometimes	Frequently	Very frequently
1 I feel uncomfortable for ages about something I've said to a colleague or they've said to me.					
2 When I tell a client what to do I expect them to do it.					
3 I work hard to get accurate information about the effectiveness of my work.					
4 When working with clients I often go with my intuition rather than stick to the rules.					
5 I smile a lot, sometimes even when I'm not saying something pleasant.					
6 I have a bit of a reputation for messing around in the office.					
7 I often say things like 'They should ...'					

Behaviour at work	Frequency				
	Almost never	*Rarely*	*Sometimes*	*Frequently*	*Very frequently*
8 If my work is boring, I try to find creative ways to make it more interesting.					
9 I often seem to know ahead of time when something is about to happen.					
10 I often wonder what clients and colleagues would do without me.					
11 I like to be spontaneous.					
12 I have no hesitation in telling my colleagues if they let me down.					
13 I work out subtle ways to get revenge on people who've harmed me.					
14 When a client is creating a crisis at work, I am known for keeping calm.					
15 I like to help others and will go out of my way to do so.					
16 I have sometimes unintentionally offended my colleagues.					
17 I look after myself and watch that I don't become too stressed.					
18 I tend to apologise too often.					

Behaviour at work	Frequency				
	Almost never	Rarely	Sometimes	Frequently	Very frequently
19 I encourage my colleagues to skive and take a long lunch with me.					
20 I like to take care of my colleagues by things like remembering their birthdays.					
21 I am sometimes late for no good reason.					

Scoring the questionnaire

Look at those questions where you have scored 'frequently' or 'very frequently'. These will be the ones which indicate your preferred 'ego state'.

Questions indicating a predominantly **Adult** ego state: 3, 14, 17
Questions indicating a predominantly **Adapted Child** ego state: 1, 5, 18
Questions indicating a predominantly **Critical Parent** ego state: 2, 7, 12
Questions indicating a predominantly **Nurturing Parent** ego state: 10, 15, 20
Questions indicating a predominantly **Rebellious Child** ego state: 13, 19, 21
Questions indicating a predominantly **Free Child** ego state: 6, 11, 16
Questions indicating a predominantly **Little Professor** ego state: 4, 8, 9

How well do you think the questionnaire highlighted your common way of behaving (your dominant ego state)? Bearing in mind what you know about ego states and their effects, it may be helpful to ask yourself the following questions and/or discuss them with a friend.

How does your predominant ego state affect:

- your stress levels at work?
- the way in which you undertake your work?
- your time management?
- your communication style?
- your relationship with colleagues and clients?

Game playing

Social workers and clients alike communicate through their own ego states. Before they've even started talking they are unconsciously playing a game, the most obvious of which is 'I'm the social worker and you're the client', and behaving accordingly. We all play psychological games regularly, if not consciously. A 'game' in this context is any regular way of behaving or interacting which covers up the real emotions or meaning behind it. Frequently, games are about poor self-esteem, avoiding taking responsibility and finding others to blame for our own inadequacies (which may not even be acknowledged to ourselves).

Table 2.2 shows some typical games and suggestions on how to overcome them.

Table 2.2   Games and how to counter them

Game	Typical player comments	Tactic
'Yes, but ...' The client plays helpless again and again, apparently asking for help but actually rejecting all sensible suggestions made by the social worker. This is a blaming game.	'Yes, I'd like to stop drinking but I can't until after Christmas.' 'Yes, I know I should play with the kids more but there's always housework to do.' 'Yes, I know I should be better with budgeting but the money always runs out by Tuesday.' 'Yes, I know I missed our appointment but I missed the bus.'	Stop offering suggestions. Ask the client what steps they need to take to improve their situation. Get the client to assess how to overcome any obstacles they have raised. Make them take responsibility for decision-making. Ask 'If you were me, what would you suggest?'
'I'm never wrong' The client cannot admit to any failing in personality or action. This means that s/he will be unwilling to listen to other viewpoints. This is a defence mechanism of someone with poor self-	'Yes, yes, I know all about that!' 'I am the best ... in my workplace.' 'Well, that's my opinion and no one's going to change it.'	Work to build up the client's self-esteem. Question the logic of their statements in a calm way. If their opinions threaten others, encourage them to see things from the others' point of view.

esteem.   *continued overleaf*

Game	Typical player comments	Tactic
'Wooden leg' The client says they cannot do something because of something earlier in their life stopping them. This is a blaming game.	'Yes, I know I don't take responsibility but it's my mother's fault.' 'I'd like a job like that but I don't come from the right sort of background.'	Encourage the client to take responsibility for their own actions. Get them to work out logical steps to reach their goals.
'Got you!' The client (and often colleagues/bosses) attempts to make you underperform by failing to give you all the information you need to do a job well. This is a poor self-esteem game.	'How could you have forgotten to do that?' 'I'm sure I told you I'd be out yesterday.' 'No, I asked you to do it *this* way.'	Take down, in writing, what you are asked to do. Summarise it verbally. If necessary, write a letter or memo confirming the action to be taken.
'The compulsive' This game is played by clients who drink or take drugs as a way of avoiding reality.	'I can handle my drink.' 'No, I'm never out of control.' 'I can stop any time I want.' 'No, I don't have a problem.'	Refer the client to a specialist unit. If they refuse to go, consider options related to referral.
'If it weren't for you' This is a blaming game in which the client avoids taking responsibility for their lack of success.	'It's all the government's fault.' 'If it weren't for you I'd have got on in my career.' 'I could cope with my life if you social workers just left me alone.'	Encourage the client to look at how their own behaviour affects their success in life. Help them to develop goal-setting skills.

Frequently we play the same games with the same people. For example, we may always play the daughter/son with our parents even though we are adult. We may always play the 'heavy-handed parent' with one type of client whilst the 'friend' with another. These variations in behaviour may be a matter of choice, but often they are unconscious – it is as if someone else is pulling our strings and off we go, following old patterns.

For social workers the trick is to recognise that they're getting caught up in the game and to find a way through. Once you know what the game is you can work out what ego state you're coming from and select another. If you realise you've been acting as a 'smother mother' to a client, change to Adult and encourage them to develop their own strategies instead of doing things for them. If you get caught in Rebellious Child with your boss, be Adult/assertive instead.

The important thing about these changes is that *they leave you in control.* If you're not in control of your mind, who is? *You* control your behaviour – you need never again kick yourself for not handling a situation in the way you prefer. If that ego state doesn't get the desired result, try another. Remember, the person with the most behaviour options is the person most likely to win.

Eric Berne's book *Games People Play* (1979) discusses many more games and how to counter them. Table 2.3 shows one last game, often played by social workers.

Table 2.3   A social worker's game

Game	Typical player comments	Tactic
'The compulsive helper' This game is played by social workers who use helping others as a way of avoiding looking at their own problems. This is a poor self-esteem game.	'Here, have my home phone number, call me any time.' 'Of course I'll lend you five pounds.' 'I don't mind visiting over the weekend.'	Look at why you are filling your life in this way. Find ways to look after yourself. Allow others to look after you occasionally.

Overcoming limiting beliefs

We have seen that much of what stops social workers being assertive is based on limiting beliefs of one sort or another – beliefs that we should act in a certain way, that we are not particular sorts of people, that this is the only way particular people can be handled. Beliefs like this limit our options and leave little room for creativity of approach. However, we *can* change these beliefs. It may take time and practice, but once the will is there, action can comfortably follow.

Exercise: Recognising and changing self-limiting beliefs

To recognise your limiting beliefs, notice what you say (or ask others to point these phrases out to you). Catch your beliefs flying by. They'll sound something like 'I'm no good at . . .', 'I can't . . .', 'I'm not the sort of person who. . .', 'I wish I had your . . .' Limiting beliefs stated out loud make you sound as if you have no control over certain areas of your life or behaviour.

However, limiting beliefs can be changed so that they become empowering by turning them into an enjoyable process to reach your goal:

- **Step 1 – Write down your limiting belief:** e.g. 'I can't say "No."'
- **Step 2 – Identify the source of this belief:** Where, when and from who did you get this belief?
- **Step 3 – Ask yourself if you are ready to change this belief:** If you don't give yourself a convincing 'Yes', identify and deal with any objections before continuing.
- **Step 4 – Ask yourself what would be more useful to believe:** Write it down or say it out loud – e.g. 'I can say "No."'
- **Step 5 – Turn it into a process:** Find something you can do to make the statement convincing (just saying the opposite won't convince you!), e.g. 'I can learn how to say "No" with practice.'
- **Step 6 – Make it enjoyable:** Find words that would make the new belief motivating (words such as 'comfortable', 'easy', 'enjoyable', 'success-fully'). Apply them to your new belief statement, e.g. 'I can enjoy learning how to say "No."' 'Developing assertiveness skills becomes easier and more exciting for me every day.'
- **Step 7 – Write down or say out loud the final version of your new belief:** Note any objections that come up (e.g. 'But I know I'll feel guilty.'). Let them go by writing them down or saying them. Work out how to over-come them. Continue until there are no further objections.
- **Step 8 – Imagine a whole day with your new belief:** Would it cause you any difficulties? If so, work out how to overcome them.
- **Step 9 – Check you now believe your final statement:** Ask yourself, 'If I could have this new belief, would I take it?'
- **Step 10 – Act 'as if' the new belief is yours:** And it will become so!

Reality is all made up – once we accept that we can make it up any way we want . . .

Source: Adapted with kind permission from John Seymour Associates Ltd, Bristol.

Exercise: Improving self-esteem

Many social workers would like to improve their self-esteem. Stated like this it is a big goal; how will you know when you've got there? By following the steps below you can work towards the 'you' you want to be:

- **Step 1 – Identify a behaviour you want to change.**
- **Step 2 – Keep a record of when, where, how and why the behaviour occurs.**
- **Step 3 – Work out how you can change the behaviour.**
- **Step 4 – Consciously behave differently until the new behaviour has been repeated approximately 20–30 times.**
- **Step 5 – Review. Has the new behaviour become automatic? If not, repeat step 4 as necessary.**

Behaviour change is difficult, you may need help to identify different ways of being. It helps to keep your goal small. Don't give yourself huge goals such as 'I'm going to be more assertive' – you will feel overwhelmed and won't know when you've reached your target. Break big goals down into manageable chunks: 'In future I will say "No" to extra work when I know I'm so busy I won't do it well.' 'In future I will ask for emotional support when I need it.' 'I will increase my ability to speak out in meetings by careful preparation. For the next two staff meetings I will say one thing, for the next two meetings I will say two things and gradually increase my contributions.' 'I will ask a trusted colleague to help me reach my goals.'

Chapter summary

There are many **barriers to assertiveness.** They include:

- **Unhelpful behaviour patterns** which were helpful at some earlier time in our life but which could now be replaced with more appropriate responses.
- **Messages we receive about our gender** – how we should behave as a woman or as a man. These messages can effectively stop us from feeling comfortable doing certain things or expressing our feelings. Indeed they can even affect how we feel in the first place.
- **Parent messages** formed in our mind by the influence of people around us as we grow up. These messages can be received verbally from what we hear said to us or about us. They can also be non-verbal, such as noticing the way our parents react to our behaviour. Parent

messages become unconscious drivers of our responses, leaving us with repetitive patterns of behaviour. Once we become consciously aware of our parent messages we can decide if we want to change them or not.

- Our **belief systems** formed from our parents' messages and what we make of life. They too are often unconscious drivers of our behaviour. Belief systems can be positive or negative. By uncovering our unconscious beliefs we can begin to change those that are un-helpful.
- **Criticism** received and how it was worded affects our self-image and self-esteem. Criticism of us as whole people is far more damaging than criticism of our behaviour alone.

Transactional Analysis offers a useful model for understanding behaviour. Eric Berne described three major ego states – the Parent, the Adult and the Child. We operate from these various states at different times and with different people depending on the situation and our interpretation of what is happening.

Most people play **games** – repetitive patterns of behaviour between two or more people. By becoming consciously aware of the game we can alter the way we habitually respond to improve our chances of getting the outcome we want.

3 Looking the part: Non-verbal communication

Whilst the words you say are obviously crucial, your non-verbal behaviour is of much greater importance in conveying messages to others than mere words alone. The staggering fact is that almost twice as much of the message you give others is non-verbal (see Figure 3.1).

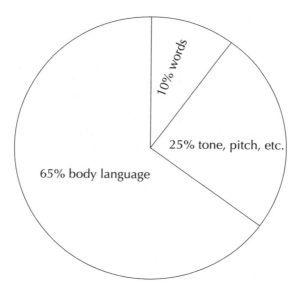

Figure 3.1   Verbal versus non-verbal communication

Non-verbal communication includes obvious things like body language, and also 'incidentals' like your clothing and hairstyle. Imagine these scenes:

- A client tells you she feels fine while looking down and having slumped shoulders.
- A colleague says he's listening to you as he picks up the phone.
- A boss says she's pleased with your work while frowning and looking tense.

Doesn't work, does it? When verbal and non-verbal messages conflict, we believe the non-verbal. Therefore it is vitally important to get this aspect of your behaviour correct (see Table 3.1).

Table 3.1   Non-verbal aspects of behaviour

	Assertive	Passive	Aggressive	Indirectly aggressive
Voice	Firm Middle pitch Warm, sincere	Quiet Too soft Whining	Loud Cold, hard Strident	Sarcastic Sharp Belittling
Speech pattern	Smooth with few hesitations Pauses for emphasis Varied tone	Hesitant, frequent pauses or speaking non-stop	Few pauses Critical words emphasised Fast	Fast Brief (often before disappearing from scene)
Facial expression	Open and approachable Smiles appropriately Frowns when displeased	Often looks away May turn mouth down at corner at end of speech	Scowls Clenched jaw Chin thrust forward Eyes 'squint'	False smile
Eye contact	Open, firm, friendly	Avoided	Staring, 'eyeballing'	Brief
Body movements	'Open' to encourage others Smooth, gestures appropriately Controls non-verbal 'leakage' Sits and stands confidently	Shoulders down and forward Head lowered Hand wringing Nervous movements	Leans forward Stands on balls of feet Walks quickly	Head on one side Leans forward

Source: Adapted from Back & Back (1982).

Cultural variations

Non-verbal communication varies vastly across cultures. Indeed it is said that only two pieces of non-verbal behaviour are universal – smiling and raising our eyebrows briefly in greeting when we approach someone. Here are a few examples of the tremendous variety across the world:

- In Turkey shaking your head means 'Yes', nodding means 'No.'
- The 'OK' gesture in English-speaking countries (thumb and first finger circled, other fingers raised) is a very rude gesture in Italy, indicates a zero in France, can mean money in Japan and a death threat in some Middle Eastern countries.
- The thumbs up signal means 'No problem' or 'Everything's OK' in Britain but in some countries such as Greece it means 'Get stuffed.'
- Women from some Middle Eastern countries do not look men in the eye.
- Different countries often have different amounts of preferred 'personal space' (how close to stand or sit next to someone else).
- Turkish men are much more likely to touch other men than is the case in Britain.

Understanding these differences can be vital to social workers, who can inadvertently offend a client from another culture, thereby damaging the working relationship. It is beyond the scope of this book to outline all possible cultural differences, and social workers dealing with people from an unfamiliar culture should get advice from their local Multi-cultural Unit or similar source.

The comments in this chapter will relate in general to white, British body language, also mentioning gender differences. We will look at individual pieces of non-verbal behaviour, but it is very important to keep in mind that one should consider the *whole* person, not just one piece of body language. **Look for clusters of non-verbal behaviour rather than relying on a single gesture**. For example, crossed arms can mean defensiveness, but can also mean the person is cold or just relaxing. You would need to take into account other parts of their non-verbal communication to make a reasoned assessment. In addition, body language should be interpreted in the light of the context in which it is displayed.

Posture

Posture often provides the strongest clue to someone's feelings, reflecting a state of mind. Stand a social worker and a depressed client side by side and what differences are you likely to see? The social worker is likely to have a relaxed, upright posture whilst a depressed client is likely to have a slumped posture with their shoulders down and forward, head lowered, and dull eyes.

Sitting postures reflect state too. Sitting relaxed, just slightly slumped and with upright head and alert eyes indicates confident interest whilst sitting with your bottom a long way forward on the seat, your legs extended and your head forward indicates an attitude of superiority. Sitting on the edge of the seat with your arms folded inward, your legs crossed and your head down could indicate nervousness.

Having a balanced and 'centred' posture is likely to reflect a feeling of stability – distributing your weight evenly whether sitting or standing. In fact, when you are standing or sitting like this you are more difficult to put off balance physically, and this will be reflected in your mental state. Expressions such as 'stand on your own two feet', 'taking a firm stand', 'so-and-so's standing in the community' reflect this poised posture. Expressions like 'I'm not sure where I stand on this' and 'shifty character' reflect an unbalanced posture and consequent image projection.

Exercise

Next time you are with other people and are not expected to be very deeply involved, watch their body language – this could be in a restaurant or other social gathering. What do you think each person is thinking or feeling? How do they feel about each other? How do they feel about what is being said? How do you feel about them? As far as possible, try to judge these points without actually listening to what is being said.

Territory

Everyone is territorial, but as we have already seen, people from different cultures require different amounts of personal space. The norm in British society is:

- **The public zone** – this is appropriate for occasions like public performances when people sit or stand at least 3.65 metres from the performer or stage.
- **The social zone** – this is the zone observed by strangers, and most people feel comfortable with a gap of around 1.25–4 metres. A familiar example of this is being on public transport. In a relatively empty train, people sit some distance from each other. As the compartment fills up

they are forced to sit in closer proximity to others. However, people attempt to retain their private zone by avoiding eye contact with those around them.

- **The casual zone** – a space of around 0.5–1.25 metres is common for casual occasions such as parties or other social gatherings. Sometimes people transgress this zone at social functions. The person who feels crowded backs away; the other person feels too distant and moves forward, and speeded up you see what appears to be one person pursuing the other around the room!
- **The intimate zone** – this begins at the body itself and extends for around 0.5 metres. This zone is usually reserved for partners and family. When anyone enters this zone, changes take place in our bodies such as increased adrenaline levels as we prepare to either run or hug. The difficulties of moving from the casual zone to the intimate zone can be observed with people who are at the early stages of becoming intimate. Movements closer are made tentatively, and first touches are usually fleeting and on a safe area of the body such as the shoulder or lower arm.

Danger – angry client!

Any type of social work is potentially dangerous. Whilst the majority of social work or probation clients pose no physical threat, most workers will at some point be confronted with people who are demented, mentally ill or violent. Learning to recognise the early danger signals given non-verbally can help workers to alter their approach or make a hasty escape. Non-verbal signals that the client is becoming angry include:

- clenched jaw
- invasion of personal space
- clenched fists (sometimes 'hidden' under their other arm or behind their back)
- 'eyeballing'
- tense posture
- restless, agitated movements
- pulse throbbing in the temple
- raised shoulders
- tapping their fingers
- avoiding eye contact
- threatening gestures such as a pointed finger
- banging their fist on the furniture or wall
- unexpected behaviour from a known client

Be aware that if your emotions are rising you may also be giving these signals and the client will pick them up at an unconscious level, possibly leading to an escalating conflict. The chapter on handling aggression has more details on this aspect of social work.

The cover-up job – detecting the lie

Jane Lyle in her book *Body Language* (Lyle, 1990) points to six categories of lies:

- **Expedience** – the 'little white lie', a lie to enable people to get along, avoid giving offence to the other person
- **Necessity** – lies used to achieve an aim, often in professional circumstances
- **Withholding** – withholding negative thoughts or falsely stating positive ones to give thinking time in a difficult situation or to enable a conversation or relationship to continue smoothly
- **Fear** – lies used when there is a fear that telling the truth will bring unwelcome consequences or punishment
- **Defence** – used to defend yourself or people you care for
- **Crime** – to cover up a misdeed

Physical reactions will vary according to how strongly the person feels about telling the lie. However, common reactions are dry mouth (leading to lip licking), nervous swallowing, and uneven breathing. Take care though – lying is not the only possible cause of these behaviours.

Jane Lyle also points out that when people are about to lie they often suddenly cross their arms and legs simultaneously. This may be an unconscious defensive movement anticipating a challenge. Tapping or moving the feet can also be a sign that someone is uncomfortable about something.

Other gestures that give away a potential lie include sitting slightly further away from you than normal, avoiding eye contact, touching the nose, or sitting stiffly and in a controlled way.

Mirroring

When people are getting along, they naturally 'mirror' each other – copy each other's body language. This is generally an unconscious process, but gives a warm feeling to the other person because it says 'I am like you' as well as 'I like you.' In Chapter 4 we explore how you can consciously use this mirroring to establish and maintain rapport with your clients and colleagues.

Exercise

Next time you're in a social situation such as a party or restaurant, watch people for mirroring. It is particularly common to see people taking a sip from their glass at the same time. Try to become more consciously aware of your own mirroring too.

Non-verbal leakage

When we are uncomfortable about something, we may be very good at covering up these feelings with our face, but the emotion tends to 'leak out' elsewhere in the body. Some of these leakage gestures such as touching the nose have just been mentioned. Hand to face gestures tend to increase when the other person is unsure of the truth of what you are saying or is lying themself. Other examples are given below, along with their possible interpretation:

- **twiddling thumbs** – often a sign of feeling bored or superior
- **tapping fingers** – impatience
- **swinging legs** – high good spirits or nervousness
- **running a hand through your hair** – either exasperation or grooming because of attraction to the other person
- **scratching yourself** – boredom
- **touching or looking at your watch** – wanting to get away
- **having one foot pointing to the door** – wanting to leave
- **touching the ear** – disbelief in what the other person is saying
- **chin rubbing** – doubting the other person
- **finger(s) in the mouth** – the person feels under pressure
- **'lint picking'** – disapproval of the speaker or what the speaker is saying
- **hands behind head** – 'I'm cleverer than you'

He says, she says – gender differences in body language

Because women and men are interacting daily, we tend not to notice gender differences in body language, but they are certainly there. Here are a few examples:

- Women tend to have less confident body language than men.
- Men take up more space than women (and not just because of bigger body size), their gestures are bigger and their posture is more extreme.
- Women are less likely than men to invade another person's body space.
- Women are more likely to lower their eyes when a conversation is difficult, and can thus appear less confident.
- Women smile more than men.
- Women fidget less and change body posture less frequently than men.

Case study – Mara

Mara, a case manager, was keen to get promoted but to date had had no luck. She felt that she wasn't treated seriously and had little influence over others. Thinking through her strengths and weaknesses she decided to take action on several fronts. One of them was her body language. A small woman, she had been socialised to sit neatly, speak quietly, smile frequently and not interrupt. She was an excellent listener and people enjoyed her company; unfortunately that didn't count for much in the promotion stakes.

There is an old saying that 'men are the natives in the workplace' (and women are the invaders). Certainly much research shows that what is inherently male (height, deeper voice tone, etc.) is more valued in British society by both women and men than what is inherently female. Taking this to heart, Mara decided to make some changes in her non-verbal presentation. She began by discarding her very casual office wear and started wearing jackets regularly – jackets are unconsciously seen as a sign of authority.

Next she decided to take up more space in meetings. She couldn't copy men by sitting too sprawled, but she could take up more space with her papers and gesture more fluently. She could sit forward more in meetings to meet others' eyes more. She also decided to smile only when appropriate; when the conversation was serious that was how she would look. She also began sitting differently, with her shoulders down, head upright and back straight.

Finally she decided to get more involved in work which would get attention. She found opportunities to give presentations. During these she moved freely, gestured more widely and generally made constructive and confident use of the space around her.

Gradually her colleagues and managers began to see her in a different light. Within a year she had the promotion she wanted.

Non-verbal communication and the interview

Social workers often have to spend time making a client feel comfortable during an interview so that they can/will speak freely. Subtly and elegantly mirroring aspects of the client's behaviour is an excellent way to do this and will be discussed in more detail in Chapter 4. However, seating is also important. If you have any choice about seating, spend some time getting this aspect right. Try to have chairs that are roughly the same height and quality. If this isn't possible, consider the effect you want to create. The person sitting in the higher, better-quality chair is unconsciously seen as superior to the person sitting in the lower chair. If you want the client to feel at ease, sit them in the 'better' chair. If you think the client may try to intimidate you, sit in the better chair yourself.

How you place the chairs is important too. Chairs placed facing each other can give a feeling of confrontation and make it difficult for the client to look away; too much eye contact can be daunting for a client talking about difficult issues. Chairs side by side are very cosy and give a feeling of intimacy (car journeys are often useful for this reason), the disadvantage being that you can't easily see the client's body language. The ideal is chairs about 1.5 metres apart and at right angles to each other – with this arrangement you can look at each other or look away comfortably.

Change your body language – change your mood

At the beginning of this chapter we saw that it is possible to give one message with your body and another with your words. The very positive side of this message is that if you change your body language deliberately, your mood will change. It is very difficult indeed to feel low for any length of time if you keep your body in an assertive stance. So what is an assertive stance?

Standing assertively

Try to imagine a string pulling you up from the centre of the top of your head. This means that you straighten your neck and spine and have your eyes facing forward (unlike the times when we were told as children to 'keep your head up' and responded by putting our heads up so high we had to look down our noses at people). Keep your shoulders low and relaxed, breathe calmly, hands relaxed and fists unclenched. Loosen any tight facial muscles. Keep your weight evenly distributed between your feet. This posture makes you look assertive and confident, and that's how you'll begin to feel.

Sitting assertively

As with standing, imagine a string pulling you up from the centre of the top of your head. This means you will sit upright, but not stiffly. Keep your shoulders low and relaxed and breathe calmly. Have your weight evenly distributed across your bottom. Legs can be crossed or uncrossed. Have arms 'open' in some way, on chair arms, or better still resting comfortably in your lap. If you're in a meeting where you're sitting around a table and it's the right height to do so, place your lower arms on the table with hands overlapping each other. This looks very businesslike.

The excellent thing about standing and sitting assertively is that as well as looking and feeling great, both postures are good for your back!

Chapter summary

Body language is even more important in the message you convey to others than the words you speak. Approximately 65 per cent of the message given is non-verbal, 25 per cent is conveyed by tone, pitch, etc., leaving 10 per cent for the actual words. This means that it is vital to have assertive body language because if you are incongruent, people will disregard your words.

- **Body language varies across cultures.** There is very little body language which is universal, in fact just a handful of gestures. Indeed some body language gestures can mean completely different things in different cultures. This means that when dealing with someone from another culture it is helpful to learn something of their non-verbal norms to avoid giving offence.
- **Men and women have different body language.** Whilst women and men are so used to being together that the differences are rarely consciously noticed, they can make a difference at an unconscious level, with women often appearing less confident and businesslike than men.
- **Mirroring** body language is a sign that two people are getting along well.
- **Non-verbal leakage,** where someone displays some gesture which is inconsistent with the rest of their body language or what they are saying, is a sign that they are uncomfortable about something. It does not tell the other person what the discomfort is, but by considering the context and conversation it may be possible to guess and probe more deeply into what is being said.
- **Office layout** can be important. Have chairs that are roughly of equal height and quality to make the client feel at ease. Place the chairs at 45 degree angles for ease of looking at or looking away during a conversation.
- **Changing your body language can change your mood.** It is very difficult to continue to feel bad if you adopt positive body language.

4 Establishing rapport

> 'Rapport – sympathetic relationship, agreement, harmony' –
> *Cassell's English Dictionary*

It is difficult to imagine being effective in the caring professions without well-developed rapport skills. Rapport skills with clients are essential because in the professional relationship they build a bridge between people of very unequal standing. Communication seems to flow smoothly when people are in rapport because both parties feel at ease; this is essential for social workers, who must enable clients to feel sufficiently at ease to talk freely about their difficulties. Suppose your client is very nervous and unsure whether to disclose information – a brisk 'I'm the professional' approach is likely to stop them speaking at all. And when dealing with a verbally aggressive client, social workers who appear timid or threatened are likely to be treated with even greater disrespect.

Social workers also need to have rapport with colleagues and those from other agencies. They must be able to negotiate for resources, mediate between warring factions, convince their boss that their decision is correct, persuade others to act on the client's behalf and carry out all the other everyday tasks within their remit.

Rapport skill 1 – clear goals

Trying to communicate without a goal in mind is like travelling without a destination – possibly enjoyable but not very productive, and you could well end up somewhere you didn't want to go. Most social workers and probation officers are well aware of the need to be goal-centred, but sometimes in long-term work this focus can be lost. Genie Laborde in her book *Influencing with*

Integrity (1994) outlines a five-step approach to keeping your communication goal-centred:

1   Aim for a specific outcome.
2   Keep positive.
3   Tune in to the other person; observe their body language and what they say.
4   Try to reach agreed goals with them.
5   Work out short- and long-term objectives.

Clients and social workers alike need to have a clear vision of the future. From this jointly agreed base you can work together, with rapport, to achieve an improved situation.

Goals should meet certain criteria:

- They must be **specific** – clearly written or articulated with no possibility of misinterpretation.
- They must be **realistic and achievable** – neither you nor the client should expect the impossible.
- They must be **measurable** – will the client know when they've got there?
- They must be **time-limited** – how long has the client got to reach the goal?

Table 4.1 gives examples of poorly formulated versus well-formulated goals.

Table 4.1   Specifying goals

Poorly formulated goals	Well-formulated goals
'You must improve your child-care soon.'	'Within the next month I want Jane to be taken to school and collected on time. She should be clean and tidy, and have breakfast before going to school.'
'You should be kinder to Joe.'	'Each time Joe cries you should give him a cuddle and talk to him gently. When he goes to bed you must read him a story.'
'I'll be better with money.'	'I will work out my incomings and out-goings, plan a budget and monitor it closely for one month, then review how I've got on.'

'I'll cut down on my drinking.'

'I'll make a chart and for the next week I'll note what I drink, when, why and how I feel. Then I'll work out a plan to alter my habits.'

Apart from the obvious requirements to comply with childcare legislation and so on, other helpful questions to help keep the goal in mind include:

- 'What will I see when I reach my goal?'
- 'What will I hear?'
- 'What will I feel?'

Clients as well as social workers can be motivated by literally having a vision of the future – a picture in their mind's eye of what life could be like. By encouraging a client to 'draw' their future in their mind, they can fine tune the picture until it becomes something they feel motivated to work towards.

Case study – Julie

Julie was a 27-year-old divorced woman with two daughters aged 6 and 3. She had drinking problems, a poorly cared for house and many debts. Life felt completely hopeless and she was seeking help.

Her desired vision of the future had several elements. She wanted to stop drinking this time (she had tried several times before and quickly lapsed). She visualised herself looking well, with clear eyes and alert mind, able to accept or reject alcohol as she chose. She also visualised herself better dressed as a result of spending less on drink. Next she visualised her daughters as happier and looking better cared for. She saw and heard herself watching television with them, chatting to them and enjoying their company. Finally, she visualised herself opening the gas bill and feeling confident that she could pay it.

Naturally, the visions in themselves were not enough; many steps were needed to achieve them. But by having that vision in mind, Julie was more easily able to get herself through the hard time ahead.

Rapport skill 2 – matching body language

When people are getting along they quite naturally 'match' each other's body language – they sit or stand in similar ways and appear to copy each other. Matching says at a subconscious level, 'I'm like you and I like you.'

Check out if you naturally match people – you probably do so unconsciously when you like the person, so you naturally possess this skill which you can develop further to put the other person at their ease. You can do this even if you don't like the other person.

You can match several different aspects of body language. Firstly you can match posture – whether the person is sitting upright or relaxed, standing erect or with their weight unevenly distributed. Next you can match arm and leg postures. Finally you can match (subtly please!) facial expressions – smile when the other person does, look serious when they do.

This matching should be done subtly and elegantly; if the other person suspects what you're doing they will probably become annoyed and distrust you. So don't match exactly but use roughly the same body language – perhaps if they have their arms folded you could just cross yours across your body; if they lean their chin on their hand you could put a hand to your face. Naturally you should match people's body language with integrity in a way that maintains respect.

Caution is needed when the other person is displaying some non-verbal gestures though. For example, if the person looks aggressive, be aware that matching this body language could escalate the temperature of the discussion. Likewise, matching a depressed person could lead to you both being depressed.

Mismatching

When people are *not* getting along, their body language will mismatch and this can be easily observed. There are times when this skill may be useful for you. Let's assume that you have been talking to someone and that you have been matching each other. If you want to end the conversation, simply begin to mismatch; the other person will get the message at an unconscious level and the discussion will quickly end.

Exercise

Find a friend to try this exercise with.

- **Step 1:** Select a subject on which you have very differing views. Spend ten minutes discussing the subject, ensuring that while you do so you match each other's body language.
- **Step 2:** Next find a topic you agree on. Discuss this for another ten minutes mismatching your body language.
- **Step 3:** When you have finished, discuss how you felt during each discussion.

You will probably find that the first discussion went much better than you would normally expect, allowing for the fact that you were in basic disagreement about the topic. Likewise, your second discussion will probably have felt more uncomfortable than you'd expect, given the level of agreement.

Pacing and leading

Pacing is when we adapt our behaviour to build rapport. Joseph O'Connor and John Seymour in their book *Introducing NLP* (1993) point out that we pace in many different ways. We match body language, tone and speed of voice to help someone feel at ease. We wear the right type of clothes to visit a client, or a different outfit to go to court. We adapt our behaviour to act respectfully to someone from a different culture. We pace emotions, sitting quietly with someone who's depressed.

Leading is when you change your behaviour to get the other person to follow you.

Using pacing and leading you can sometimes turn around a person's mood by manipulating *their* body language. Suppose someone is looking tense or depressed. At the beginning of the discussion match their body language (pacing) for a while until you feel that rapport has been established, then subtly alter your body language (leading) to a more positive and assertive one (or a more relaxed one, whichever is appropriate). Hopefully, they will follow your lead and, as we saw in Chapter 3, where the body goes the mood usually follows.

Exercise

- **Step 1:** For a few days, observe other people in conversation, looking for examples of matching.
- **Step 2:** For the next few days, observe your own body language, noting when you are matching the person you are speaking to.
- **Step 3:** Select some relatively unimportant and unthreatening situations in which to practise matching the person you are speaking to.
- **Step 4:** Again, in a non-threatening situation, practise pacing and leading a client during an interview.

Rapport skill 3 – matching the spoken word

We have seen in Chapter 3 that approximately 65 per cent of our message is given non-verbally, an additional 25 per cent being given by our tone, pitch and speed of delivery. There is a great range of possible voice tones or tempos, just as there are a great variety of accents.

The vocal range of women and men overlaps quite a lot and it is true that sometimes tone is culturally defined. Likewise rhythm and speed of delivery can vary across cultures and indeed from one part of the country to another. Imagine if you will the quick delivery of a Birmingham accent compared with the soft burr of a Norfolk one. These differences can lead to people from quick-speaking cultures believing that those from slow-speaking cultures are in some way slow-witted. People from slow-speaking cultures can think that fast-speaking people are always in a hurry.

Tones can be loud, soft, high or low. To be effective you don't have to match people's tone exactly, of course. For example, a woman with a high-pitched voice would have difficulty matching a man with a very low-pitched voice but may be able to make minor adjustments towards what is natural for the other person. Remember how Margaret Thatcher learned to lower her tone to better match the man's world in which she moved?

Tempos can be fast or slow, with or without pauses. People who naturally speak very quickly can sometimes feel impatient with slow speakers and finish their sentences for them. Slow speakers can feel overwhelmed by the speed of the other person's delivery and simply give up the effort. By adjusting your speed to match the other person's they will feel more comfortable with you and your rapport will deepen.

Matching language

As well as matching tone and pitch, you can increase rapport by using the same type of language as the other person. Listen for whether people use short words and short sentences or if their speech is more complex. By matching such speech patterns the other person will again get the message, 'I'm like you and I like you.' Along with this type of matching, make sure you only use jargon or specialised terms where the other person would easily understand their meaning. These skills are particularly important for people in the caring professions, who tend to be much better educated than their clients and who, like every other profession, have their own jargon and abbreviations.

Rapport skill 4 – talking in categories

It hardly needs saying that different people like to talk about different things. What we don't always register, though, is that different people talk about different things in different ways. Think about a keen cinemagoer – what aspect of the film does the person talk about? The cinema itself? The actors? The action in the film? The way in which the film is directed? The cost of making the film? The emotions aroused by the film? How it compared with what the critics said?

If you can learn to identify the categories in which people talk and be sufficiently flexible in your approach to match these categories, the other person will feel more at ease. So what categories might people use? Here are some suggestions; you may think of others:

- Other people
- Self
- Places
- Things
- Activities
- Numbers
- Money
- Time
- Feelings
- Ideas
- Technology
- The past
- Facts

Exercise

For a few days consciously take note of the categories preferred by people with whom you closely interact. Then review a few of the conversations, assessing how you could match their categories. When you feel confident you can do this, try it out. Once you have gained this skill in 'safe' situations you will be ready to use it in the social worker–client relationship.

Rapport skill 5 – sensitivity to difference

In Chapter 3 we saw that non-verbal communication is culturally bound – there is very little body language that is universal. Thus speaking to people from different cultures presents additional rapport challenges. It may well not be possible to match their body language in detail but you can match general stance and a small selection of their movements. More importantly, try to avoid any body language or dress that would offend – if in doubt check out cultural norms before you visit a new client from an unfamiliar culture.

Likewise remember that there are many different gender differences in communication. Deborah Tannon in her book *You Just Don't Understand* (1990) says that whilst most female communication is based on co-operation, most male communication is based on hierarchy. 'Hierarchy' here means the need to be one up or at least not one down. Social work clients are, by the nature of the very relationship basis, in a one down position. In addition, social workers are often younger and better educated than their clients. These and other factors mean that the client can be on the defensive before you even knock on the door.

Rapport skill 6 – matching representational systems

Social workers spend a lot of time listening to clients and are often trained in this important skill. Their task is to encourage the speaker to continue by using active listening skills – looking at the speaker a lot, matching, nodding, saying 'Go on' and so on. The speaker (as in any conversation) looks at the listener but also looks away when thinking what to say next. Interestingly, *where* the person looks is an indicator of *how* the person has stored the information they are trying to retrieve.

Think about the last time you dealt with a difficult client. How did you represent that memory in your mind? Did you visualise the scene? Did you hear what was said? Did you feel again what you felt at the time? Did you smell any odours that were present? Did you think through the conversation logically through internal dialogue? You may have experienced one or more of these ways of retrieving a memory.

Different people store data in different ways. Some people use internal dialogue, some are predominantly visual, some are aural, some are kinaesthetic (feelings) whilst a few are predominantly olfactory (smell). This is known as a person's representational system – the way they represent information in their mind. There are no right or wrong ways to store and retrieve information, just differences between individuals. Just as with other matching, if you can work out how people store and retrieve information you can match them and increase rapport by changing your language to suit their representational systems.

There are two ways to work out a person's representational system. First, you can just listen to their expressions. Here are some examples:

- **Visual representation:**
    - 'Well, as I see it ...'
    - 'That brings to mind a picture of ...'
    - 'I see what you mean.'
    - 'It appears to me ...'
- **Auditory representation:**
    - 'That sounds to me like ...'
    - 'As I hear it ...'

- – 'That's unheard of.'
- – 'In a manner of speaking.'

- **Kinaesthetic (feelings):**

  - – 'I feel that . . .'
  - – 'It touches me when . . .'
  - – 'Hold on a minute . . .'

- **Inner dialogue:**

  - – 'I think that . . .'
  - – 'Logically . . .'
  - – 'Let's consider . . .'

- **Olfactory:**

  - – 'I smell a rat.'
  - – 'I was left with a bitter taste in my mouth.'

Joseph O'Connor and John Seymour's book *Introducing NLP* (1993) has a more comprehensive list of sensory-based language.

The second is to watch where their eyes move when they are thinking what to say next. Because different representational systems are located in different parts of the brain, when we are retrieving information from certain areas our eyes move in certain directions. Figure 4.1 shows the eyes of a person *as you look at them* (not your own) and would apply to a right-handed person; left-handed people's eyes often move in the opposite direction. This is not an infallible guide, but a good generalisation. Underneath each pair of eyes is an explanation and a sample question you could ask that would typically get the person's eyes to move in that direction. But remember, they may not do so because, despite the wording of your question, they may retrieve information in a different way.

In any conversation people will use a mixture of these representational modes, and they will frequently use more than one when thinking of the answer to a single question – they see the picture, hear the words that went with it and feel what they felt. However, you can usually note that people use one mode more than another. When you have observed this you can change your language to match their mode and strengthen rapport. Here are some examples of words and phrases suited to each of the representational systems:

- **Visual** – look, see, focus, foresee, illustrate, bright, watch, visualise, blinkered view, colourless personality, it appears to me, in my mind's eye, eyeing up, I see what you mean, looking at it from all points of view

Eyes straight ahead = general visualisation mode
In this case the person is 'seeing' an image.
'How do you see that?'

Eyes up right = visual remembered
In this case the person is recalling something they have actually seen in the past.
'How did your child look the last time you smacked him?'

Eyes up left = visual constructed
In this case the person is constructing a new image they have never seen before.
'How would you look if you stopped drinking?'

Eyes to the side right = aural remembered
In this case the person is remembering something they have heard in the past.
'What did he say then?'

Eyes to the side left = aural constructed
In this case the person is constructing a new sound they have not heard before.
'What could you say to the Benefits Agency?'

Eyes down left = kinaesthetic
Here the person is aware of feelings and bodily sensations.
'How do you feel about that?'

Eyes down right = internal dialogue
The person is 'talking to themselves'.
'What do you think about that?'

Figure 4.1   Eye movement and representational systems

- **Auditory** – hear, loud, clear, I hear what you say, as I hear it, it sounds like, that rings a bell, you're coming across loud and clear, unheard of
- **Olfactory** – smells like, a fishy tale, fresh, stale, a taste for ..., sweet person, bitter memory
- **Kinaesthetic** – in touch with, I feel, you must feel, smooth as silk, rough, heavy as lead, tension, pressure, stress, I grasp what you mean, just scratching the surface
- **Inner dialogue** – I think, I'll consider it, I understand what you mean, process, I need to decide that, I recognise your viewpoint

By the way, if you simply ask people what their dominant representational mode is they may well not know. For example, in some people visualisations are just outside conscious awareness, yet ask them a simple question like 'Imagine an apple, what colour is it?' and they'll be able to tell you!

Chapter summary

- **Goal setting** is a very important rapport skill when working with clients. By knowing where you are going, how to measure results and when deadlines are you can avoid much miscommunication and irritation. Goals should always be written in a positive form, aiming *towards* something rather than *away from* something: 'I will spend an hour playing happily with the children' rather than 'I won't shout at the children for an hour.' Clients can be motivated towards their goals by being encouraged to see, hear and feel what life will be like when they reach them.
- **Matching body language:** When people get along they naturally tend to copy each other's body language. You can do this deliberately to increase the amount of comfort others feel with you.
- **Matching tone of voice:** Just as with body language, matching tone of voice can lead to a feeling of mutuality.
- **Matching speed of delivery:** Speed up or slow down your speech to match the other person; it will increase how comfortable they feel with you.
- **Matching categories:** Notice how people talk about things. Do they like to talk about money, numbers, people, coincidences, objects? Match your conversation to theirs and rapport will increase greatly.
- **Matching representational systems:** By observing eye movements and listening to someone's words you can work out if they predominantly represent their world to themselves through pictures, words, logic or feelings. By choosing the words you use accordingly you can make the other person feel more at ease.

5 Your rights as a social worker and as an individual

Our belief systems are so ingrained by the time we are adults, our parent messages so firmly embedded, that it can seem sometimes as if we have no right to change, to look after ourselves and our needs. We may not believe this on an intellectual level, but the unwanted behaviour nevertheless continues as if it were outside our control. Social workers, who are well aware of their clients' rights and how to fight for them, may overlook their own rights because most of them are not part of any policy or legislation. They often take more care of their clients' rights than they do of themselves.

Your rights as an individual

Assertive rights are not written down in policy or in law but are about believing that we have the right to look after ourselves and our needs whilst respecting others. Think of it this way. Perhaps you don't like complaining when you're dissatisfied with something you've purchased. However, you do know that you have consumer rights and could check with a Citizens' Advice Bureau what they are. Armed with this knowledge you might feel more confident about returning the faulty goods.

Likewise you will be aware that as a citizen you have certain legal rights. If a neighbour moves their fence onto your land you could check your legal rights and more confidently speak to them about it. Or if your boss suddenly said you could only have three weeks' holiday instead of four you could look up your contractual rights before disagreeing.

Believing in your rights gives confidence in tackling situations.

Assertive rights are about believing that you and others have certain rights simply as human beings, and they stem from the right to be treated with respect. Let's look at a typical list of assertive rights and the responsibilities that go with each right. Table 5.1 is not comprehensive – you may think of other rights applicable to your own situation.

Table 5.1   Assertive rights as an individual

Right	Responsibility
I have the right to be treated with respect.	I must act respectfully towards others.
I have the right to say 'No' without feeling overwhelmed with guilt.	I must let the other person know my message clearly and without hurt.
I have the right to be listened to.	I do not have the right to expect others to agree with me, and I will accept the consequences of stating my views.
I have the right to ask for what I want.	I must accept that sometimes people will refuse my request.
I have the right to make mistakes.	I will learn from the mistakes and try to avoid them in future.
I have the right to select my behaviour style.	I will not knowingly disrespect others.

Commonly, people accept their rights at an intellectual level, but at a behavioural and feeling level the story is very different. Check whether you *really* accept your rights by asking yourself:

- Do I back down when the situation becomes difficult?
- Do I feel guilty when I have stood up for myself?
- Do I have to plan carefully and grit my teeth before speaking to someone about an issue involving my rights?
- Do I naturally remember this right or keep having to remind myself of it?

How beliefs affect out attitude to rights

Figure 5.1 demonstrates how our attitude to rights is affected by our belief systems and vice versa, one reinforcing the other unless we take conscious action to break out of the circle. Before we look at these rights in more detail it is important to remember that **these rights are for everyone.** This reflects the fact that being assertive is not about getting your own way all the time. Respecting your rights and the rights of others often calls for compromise.

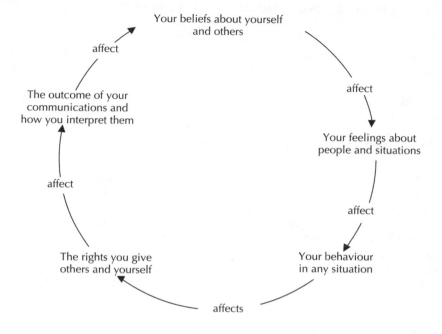

Figure 5.1   Rights and beliefs cycle

Source: Adapted from Back and Back (1982) *Assertiveness at Work,* reproduced with kind permission of McGraw-Hill Companies.

The difference is that by acting assertively you will come to a *workable compromise* – one which is the best possible solution for everyone – as opposed to *compromising yourself,* where you betray your beliefs and feel badly about yourself afterwards.

The right to be treated with respect

Many people say that respect must be earned, but this is looking at respect from a slightly different perspective. Social workers will be familiar with the idea of respecting people no matter what their behaviour. It is about separating the person from the behaviour. You may totally abhor the fact that the person in front of you sexually abused their child, but if you treat them with disrespect you will never achieve a satisfactory working relationship. Likewise you have the right to be treated with respect even if you've done something you'd rather forget. No one's perfect!

The right to say 'No' without feeling overwhelmed with guilt

Most people struggle with saying 'No' and this is hardly surprising. As children we get little practice at saying 'No' in an assertive way and are often forbidden to say it to adults. Saying 'No' to parents may have brought about a telling off, a smack or, even more devastating, withdrawal of love for a period. Add to this the pressure to be helpful and co-operative (especially for women) and there is real difficulty in making a refusal assertively, if at all.

The right to be listened to

Many passive people struggle with this right. They may have had strong parent messages as a child to be seen and not heard. They may have come from a family that didn't communicate much, or believed that certain subjects should not be discussed. If you feel you are not being listened to, you have the right to stop the other person in their tracks and request that they listen while you repeat your message. Chapter 3 on body language will help you give a congruent message. Of course, in return you must be a good listener; this right is not about taking up all the available communication time.

The right to ask for what you want

How many of us had parents who said, 'Those that ask don't get,' and conversely, 'Those that don't ask don't want.' A no-win situation: we grow up believing that we shouldn't ask for anything for ourselves; for our clients yes, but not for ourselves. Furthermore, having to ask for something shows that we can't manage in some way. Perhaps we worry that our line manager won't think us competent if we ask for a co-worker on a difficult case. Perhaps we worry it will affect our promotion prospects if we refuse to make home visits to a client we believe to be dangerous. It is also very common indeed for people not to ask for clarification in group situations. How often have you sat in a meeting or at a course and not understood something but said nothing?

The right to make mistakes

We all make mistakes, none of us is perfect, yet many of us feel terrible about the most simple error. We do a big cover-up job or we go around telling everyone, wanting them to make us feel better. Do your best, accept that you will occasionally make mistakes, learn from them and get on with your life.

The right to select your behaviour style

In Chapter 1 we discussed the fact that the person with the most behaviour options is the person most likely to succeed. Sometimes you may choose to act passively or aggressively for a purpose. However, by making the choice rather than simply letting your feelings get the better of you, you have continued to behave assertively. You will be able to tell the difference by how you feel afterwards. If you have simply not stood up for yourself or lost your temper you'll probably be kicking yourself afterwards; if you've made a decision to be passive or aggressive you'll continue to feel in control.

Exercise

Identify some rights you would like for yourself which will not infringe others' rights (although perhaps some negotiation would be necessary). Some examples might be:

- having some time to myself
- getting the family to do their share of the housework
- buying myself some flowers when I'm down
- not visiting my mother when she annoys me
- not answering the phone in the middle of a meal

Your rights as a social worker

In addition to individual rights, you can consider what assertive rights may apply to you as a worker. Some examples are given in Table 5.2 overleaf.

Table 5.2   Workers' rights

Rights	Responsibilities
To expect reasonable work from others	To do good work myself and tell others if I'm unhappy with their work
To expect good supervision from my manager	To say what I want from supervision and go to the meeting well prepared
To work reasonable hours	To have good time management skills and say 'No' to excess work
Not to be given work which is too difficult for my experience and skill level	To tell my manager if I think I can't do a piece of work well
To have a lunch break	To take a lunch break
To get feedback on my work from my line manager	To ask for feedback if necessary
To be listened to in meetings	To be prepared for the meeting and state my case succinctly
To get support from other professionals	To ask for support if necessary and provide support in return
To refuse to see clients alone when I feel there is potential danger	To make my case clearly and with all possible supporting evidence
To expect that there is immediate response to the 'panic button'	To check where the panic button is and that it is in good working order

The right to expect a reasonable standard of work from others

It can be very difficult to criticise colleagues who aren't pulling their weight, but of course failing to do so would be to ignore your own rights. By causing extra work for you they infringe your rights. Keeping this in mind should encourage you to speak out for yourself. In Chapter 8 we will discuss how to give a difficult criticism in a constructive way.

The right to expect good supervision from your manager

It can be very difficult to challenge an underperforming manager – there's a lot at stake. Managers not only supervise; they recommend for upgrading and give references. However, your reputation is at stake and poor supervision affects your ability to work effectively. Your responsibility is to go well prepared to supervision. Know exactly what you need; state it clearly, letting your manager know that it will reflect well on him/her if you do well, and be persistent until you get what you need (see Chapter 8 on giving criticism).

The right to work reasonable hours

Social workers of any description are prone to working long or irregular hours – it's in the nature of the task. But a few social workers become a martyr to the job, working evenings and weekends, whilst others manage to keep their hours more regular. If this sounds like you, you could be failing to respect yourself, and your responsibility is to make sure that you don't work so long that you work poorly or become ill.

The right not to be given work which is too difficult for your experience or skill level

It is commonplace for social workers (particularly newly qualified staff) to be quickly given work that pushes their limits. It can be tempting to take the work on – you're given an opportunity to prove yourself and the work may be interesting. However, difficult work done badly helps neither you nor the client. Your responsibility is to assess carefully whether you can do the work, and quickly ask for help if necessary.

The right to have a lunch break

Research shows that people who fail to take a lunch break get no more work done because they work less efficiently for the rest of the day. You would give your clients advice to look after themselves in this way; do it for yourself.

The right to get feedback on work from your line manager

Hopefully, you will be receiving regular feedback via supervision and your appraisal system. However, some managers are not good at giving clear messages, and it can be daunting to ask in case the news is bad. But without this information it's difficult for you to assess your progress. Your responsibility is to ask directly for feedback as required.

The right to be listened to in meetings

Social workers and others commonly complain that they don't feel listened to in meetings. The type of meetings social workers attend are often populated by professional people well used to making their point. Chapter 3 on body language gives useful tips on non-verbal ways to be listened to in meetings. Your responsibility is to prepare for the meeting, plan the points you want to get across, and state them as thoroughly and succinctly as possible.

The right to get support from other professionals

Field social workers in particular are often working as part of a professional team, but the reality is that some personnel can be very difficult to work with – they don't attend meetings or keep you informed of developments. Your responsibility is to keep them informed and ask for support as required. Naturally you would offer support in return.

The right to refuse to see clients alone when you feel in danger

Field social workers and probation officers in particular face making home visits in hostile housing areas and with potentially aggressive clients. Sometimes managers press for these dangerous visits to be made alone because of staff shortages. Your responsibility is to look after your safety – speak to your union representative if you feel pressured by your manager and have tried explaining your viewpoint without result. See Chapter 11 on handling aggressive people for further information on this type of situation.

The right to have the panic button answered immediately

In many social work and probation offices 'panic button' systems are far from perfect. Either they are non-existent, don't work or produce little response. You have every right to expect help immediately. Your responsibility is to check the panic button system and if necessary raise the issue with management to have the system improved.

Exercise

Think back over the past week or two to events in your life. Have there been times when you have violated other people's rights? If so, how did this occur and what steps can you take to prevent the situation being repeated?

Were there times when your rights were violated by others? If so, were you happy with how you handled the situation, or is there anything you would change? How did the situation occur, and what steps can you take to prevent this happening again?

Your rights as a manager

As a social work manager you have many duties and responsibilities. One of them is to look after the rights of your staff; another important one is to look after yourself. In fact, all of the rights listed for social workers also apply to yourself. However, as a manager you have additional rights and responsibilities, some of which are listed in Table 5.3.

Table 5.3   Managers' rights

Rights	Responsibilities
To chair meetings effectively	To prepare for the meeting, keep to time and allow everyone to have their rightful say
To expect a good standard of work from my staff	To give full support and training, and not overload staff
Not to be overworked	To be realistic about how much work I can do – managers commonly overwork, often doing many more hours than their staff

The right to chair meetings effectively

Social work staff and managers spend a lot of time in meetings and a lot of it gets wasted. As the chairperson you have an opportunity to ensure that time is well spent. Chairing meetings effectively involves:

- being clear about the purpose of the meeting
- ensuring that everyone present is necessary
- ensuring that everyone necessary is present
- taking control of the meeting
- taking notes or minutes, or delegating this task to someone else
- encouraging people to be punctual
- allowing people to attend only for that part of the meeting that affects them
- giving quiet people an opportunity to have their say
- keeping overtalkative people in control
- reaching decisions within the group

The right to expect a good standard of work from your staff

Many managers steer clear of criticising their staff, fearing that it may cause resentment and difficult working relationships. However, it is your right (and the client's right) to expect work to be done correctly. Furthermore, you are doing your staff member a disservice by allowing poor work; it will affect their self-esteem, their reputation and career prospects.

It is possible to respect your subordinate's rights and correct their work at the same time by approaching them from the perspective of a Nurturing Parent rather than a Critical Parent (see Chapter 2). The section in Chapter 8 on giving criticism shows some strategies for this difficult task.

The right not to be overworked

A report recently showed that most managers had 40 hours' work on their desk at any one time; a daunting thought. If this is true for you, you must take active steps to protect your rights and reduce your stress levels.

Are you delegating enough? Delegation is when you train your staff to take on some of your work, as opposed to work allocation when you give staff work which is normally theirs. Many managers hesitate to delegate because their staff are so hard pressed or because they believe the work will not be done well. Nevertheless, there are several reasons why delegation might safeguard your rights and those of your staff:

- The work might get done quicker.
- The staff member may already possess the skills and can get the work done efficiently without training.
- The staff member will develop additional skills to motivate them and/or further their career.

Frequently when managers finally begin to delegate they are pleasantly surprised that their staff somehow find time in a busy schedule to take on a working party, write a report or some other interesting and different task. Of course you may initially give yourself more work while you train up the subordinate, but in the long run you'll save time and energy.

Exercise: Other people's rights

Consider any difficulty you have in respecting other people's rights, for example:

- **Self-determination** – do you get upset when your partner wants to wash up later than you want it done, even though there's no practical reason for a particular timeframe?
- **Assertiveness** – do you feel irritated when a client stands up to you even if they're right?
- **Success** – do you find it difficult to accept a sincere complement from others?
- **Confidentiality** – do you find yourself talking about cases to people outside your organisation?

Try to work out why any areas are difficult for you. Is there some problem from your childhood, or do you lack support in some way? Make an action plan to develop your skills in this area to ensure that you are fully respecting others' rights.

Exercise: My additional rights as a manager

Spend a few minutes identifying additional rights which you have as a manager. Then plan active steps towards achieving these rights.

Exercise: My rights

Here is an exercise to help you assess your comfort with standing up for your rights in future:

1   I find it difficult to ask for ....

    ....

    from ....

    In the past I dealt with this by ....

    ....

In future I will remember I have the right to ....

and will deal with this situation by ....

....

2   Last time someone made fun of me I responded by ....

....

In future I will remember I have to right to...

and will deal with this situation by ....

....

3   Last time I disagreed with the majority view in a meeting I ....

....

and I felt ....

In future I will remember I have to right to...

and will deal with this situation by ....

....

4   When I say 'No' I often feel ....

In future I will remember I have to right to ....

and will deal with this situation by ....

....

5   When I have to say something difficult to a client I ....

....

and I feel ....

In future I will remember I have to right to ....

and will deal with this situation by ....

....

6   When colleagues do not give me adequate support I ....
and I feel ....
In future I will remember I have to right to ....
and will deal with this situation by ....
....

7   The last time a client treated me with disrespect I ....
and I felt ....
In future I will remember I have to right to ....
and will deal with this situation by ....
....

8   When people ignore my opinion I ....
and I feel ....
In future I will remember I have to right to ....
and will deal with this situation by ....
....

9   When I make a mistake I ....
and I feel ....
In future I will remember I have to right to ....
and will deal with this situation by ....
....

10 When I am asked to take on too much work I ....
and I feel ....
In future I will remember I have to right to ....
and will deal with this situation by ....
....

Chapter summary

- Many social workers are aware of their clients' rights and know how to fight for them. However, **they sometimes fail to stand up for their own rights.**
- **Assertive rights** stem from a belief that you and others have the right to be treated with respect. Relating the usefulness of assertive rights to other rights you have, such as legal or contractual rights, can convince you that belief in these rights will be of value to you.
- **Rights are for everyone** – they are not a charter for selfishness. This means that you will often have to reach a workable compromise. This involves arriving at the best possible win–win solution to a situation. It does not mean compromising yourself and your integrity.
- **All rights carry a responsibility.**

6 Making requests

Many people become angry and stressed because they don't get enough of what they want. Social workers are no different from their clients in this respect – they also have wants and needs which, if left unsatisfied, produce lower morale and lost motivation.

Professionally, social workers want:

- their profession to be regarded with respect by the media and the public
- their expertise to be recognised
- adequate pay for a difficult job
- resources to do the job properly

As individuals, social workers want:

- proper supervision
- support from peers, management and their organisation
- a realistic caseload
- safety from physical violence
- adequate training to do their job well

One major reason why people don't get what they want is simply because they don't ask for it. People often sabotage their chances of having their needs met because some aspect of their belief system gets in the way. These belief systems often involve an expectation that the other person should be a mind reader:

- 'If he was any sort of manager he'd know I need help to do . . .'
- 'If she was a decent colleague she'd know that I need someone to talk to right now.'

- 'She is deliberately withholding that information from me.'
- 'No one tells me anything.'
- 'No one noticed I handled that situation really well.'
- 'She shouldn't send me to deal with that man, he's known to be violent.'

This expectation of mind reading is even more powerful with those we love – 'If s/he really loved me s/he'd ...' But conversely, we get irritated if others expect us to mind read: 'Well, how could I know that's what she wanted, I'm not a mind reader, am I?'

So we go around moaning to ourselves and others that we are hard done by when the fault lies within ourselves and our failure to communicate clearly.

Exercise

To check how confident you are about getting your needs met, complete the simple questionnaire below.

Need to be met	Comfort level (1 = v. uncomfortable 10 = v. confident)	What stops me feeling confident
Asking a colleague to take on some work for you		
Asking your line manager for some time off		
Asking a client to turn off the television		
Asking a colleague to refrain from smoking in your car		
Asking a police officer to escort you to a house		
Asking the court for more time to prepare and report		
Asking the family of an elderly person to give the person more time to make a decision about their future		

Asking is difficult

Asking for what we want is often difficult because we may have received powerful messages as children not to do so. We may have been told things like: 'Don't ask for anything when you're at your friend's house!' 'Don't say "I want".' 'Wait to be offered.' 'Those that ask don't get.' Non-verbally, we may simply have had our requests ignored, training us to stop expecting anything for ourselves.

Women in particular are socialised to look after the needs of others, often putting them before their own needs. They give men the best cuts of meat, spend money on their children before themselves, help the community until their energy runs out.

A refusal is just a refusal – not a personal rejection

Another reason why asking is difficult is because we fear that the other person won't be able to refuse assertively, and we'll feel rejected. Worse still, they may refuse us aggressively, leaving us hurt and bewildered. But it's worth remembering that when someone says 'No' they are simply refusing a request, not rejecting you as a whole person.

Alternatively we may worry that the person may say 'Yes' when they want to say 'No' because they aren't assertive enough to look after their needs, so we have to look after them as well as ourselves.

An end to moaning

One possibility is to resolve that each time you find yourself moaning about a situation (whether to yourself or others), you will work towards finding one solution to the problem. You could help empower others to do the same by asking questions like, 'What would you rather have?' 'How can that be avoided?' 'Is there anything we can do?' each time a person slips into 'poor me' mode, complaining as if they have no power to alter their situation.

Those that ask *do* get

The comedian John Cleese does a sketch showing the difference between the English and Americans asking someone to pass the salt at the dinner table. Whilst the American simply says, 'Please pass the salt,' the English person says, 'I wonder ... would you mind awfully ... I'm sorry to trouble you but ...

could you pass me the salt?' An exaggeration of course, but as with all good humour, one with a large grain of truth embedded in it.

The truth is that those who ask are more likely to get what they want, simply because others will be aware of their needs. It is your right to ask for what you want. If this seems too bold, remember that it is the other person's right to say 'No.'

Giving clear request messages

To make requests clearly involves a number of steps:

- **Step 1** – Decide what you want.
- **Step 2** – Decide who to ask.
- **Step 3** – Consider the effects of the request on the other person.
- **Step 4** – Decide when to ask.
- **Step 5** – Decide how to ask.

Step 1: Decide what you want

This sounds terribly obvious, but it sometimes happens that we are much clearer about what we *don't* want rather than what we *do* want.

Case study – Sarah

Sarah has been qualified two years, and for the past few months has been increasingly unhappy in her work. She realises that she has been handling this dissatisfaction badly, moaning to colleagues and her partner without taking any active steps to rectify the situation. She decides to sit and write a list of things that she's unhappy about, and then write what she wants instead (see Table 6.1).

Table 6.1   Sarah's list

Don't like	Want instead	Steps to take
lack of clear career progression	clarification of steps to take to further my career	speak to my line manager and personnel
feeling pressured to take on too much work	a clear understanding by my boss of the work I have in hand	list all my cases and estimate the amount of time spent on each
sharing a phone line with three others	my own phone line	raise the matter at every team meeting and if necessary write to the director

By working through her wants and needs systematically, Sarah can begin to feel in control of the situation. She can work out what she can directly alter by asking for what she wants, and also find ways to influence others who have the power to give her what she needs.

Step 2: Decide who to ask

It is clearly no good asking the wrong person for something. It is no good asking a colleague for resources over which they have no control, for example. It is no good asking an elderly, demented person to tell you when she needs help. Sometimes you also have to accept that whilst some people may have the power to grant your request, they may be unwilling to do so. In this case you may have to find another way to get your needs met.

Step 3: Consider the effects of the request on the other person

Will your request put the other person under too much pressure? Will they be flattered to be asked to help? What might be in it for them to say 'Yes' to you?

If we look at Sarah's situation again, all three of her requests will have effects on others:

- *Career progression* – working towards this means that she will almost certainly have to take on some different work – and by implication stop doing some things she is doing now. This will impact on her team and her line manager.
- *Being clear about not taking on too much work* – this is almost certainly very sensible. Taking on too much work makes people stressed and often means that the work is not done properly. However, from the line manager's viewpoint, Sarah's need for a reasonable caseload means that more unallocated cases will stack up.
- *Sharing a phone line* – whilst everyone agrees this is necessary, Sarah's line manager may think the effort involved in pressurising for the funding for this is low on the list of priorities.

By using empathy in this way you will show respect for the other person and their needs, and also anticipate any objections that could be raised to your request.

Step 4: Decide when to ask

Asking somebody for something when they are busy, tired or irritable is more likely to bring a negative result than approaching them when they are calm, unhurried and have time to consider your request properly. This most basic principle is often overlooked when people make requests.

Step 5: Decide how to ask

Some requests are simple: 'I'd like to leave early today please.' In this case make your requests simply and in an active voice: 'I'd like...', 'I want...' and so on. In other words, use the word 'I' rather than make vague statements such as, 'Wouldn't it be nice if we...' or 'Perhaps we could...' But if agreeing to your request is likely to require thought or consequences for the other person, you will need to think through your strategy in advance. Chapter 12 on negotiating offers further advice on this topic.

In Sarah's case she decides to speak to her line manager during supervision about her caseload. She runs through the scene in her mind, visualising each step and rehearsing what she will say and how Peter, her line manager, might respond:

Sarah: *'Peter, I need to speak to you about two issues. Firstly, I have been checking my work and find that five childcare cases are taking 75 per cent of my time, I can show you the figures if you like. I have realised that I feel uncomfortable during supervision because you ask me indirectly if I can take on more work. I do understand the pressure you're under having to hold these cases and deal with them on a duty basis, but I want to let you know that I can't take on any more. My second point is that I've been thinking about my career development. There are still one or two types of work I haven't undertaken yet and I feel this will affect my chances of getting promotion when I apply for jobs. Can we do something about this?'* (Note that Sarah has consistently used active 'I' messages throughout this conversation.)

Peter: *So you're asking me to give you different work when there's ten unallocated childcare cases?*

Sarah: (respecting Peter's point of view) *'I realise that's really difficult for you but I wonder if there's a way round it. Could we scan the referrals and if necessary pick cases that don't look like they would take too much time? I could just work on one at a time and closely monitor how many hours they take.'*

Peter: *'But the type of work you're talking about doesn't come into the team very often.'*

Sarah: (having checked her facts before speaking) *'Yes, I thought of that. I was speaking to Jim in East team and he'd like some more experience of direct work with children. I wonder if he could take on a piece of work for me in return for me taking a case from his team?*

Peter: *'I'll need some time to think about this.'*

Sarah: (respecting his need but aware of the need to keep her goal time-limited) *'I understand. Could we schedule this for discussion at our next supervision session?'*

This request is more likely to work because Sarah has been modest in what she's asked for. She hasn't asked to have existing work taken off her, and has backed up her request for no more childcare cases at present with hard statistics. Furthermore, she's only asking to take on one additional different case at a time, and if necessary she will swap some work with Jim from East team. She has respected her manager's needs as well as her own.

The 'Broken Record' technique

'Broken Record' is an excellent technique to use when the other person either won't hear you or tries to deflect what you are saying. It is a very simple and effective technique when people won't take 'No' for an answer, don't listen to your point in meetings, or in any other situation where you need to make your point strongly.

'Broken Record' is so named because it involves repeating your message several times. Here is a step by step approach:

- **Step 1** **Decide your goal.**
- **Step 2** **State your case, including your 'Broken Record' statement.**
- **Step 3** **Listen to what the other person has to say and decide if you will change your mind.**
- **Step 4** **If you have not changed your mind, respond briefly to their comment and then repeat your 'Broken Record' statement.**
- **Step 5** **Repeat steps 3 and 4 up to five times.**

If the other person raises an important issue, but one which is not immediately relevant to the topic, simply say: 'That's important, we'll discuss that in a minute, but now I ...'

Let's imagine that Sarah is concerned about one of her clients, a young boy called Sean. She is concerned that he may have slight developmental delay, but the GP has so far fobbed her off and done nothing about a full assessment. Sarah decides to phone Dr Patel:

Sarah: *'Hello Dr Patel, it's Sarah Barnet from South team here. I need to speak to you for a few minutes about a case. Is this a good time?'* (She respects the doctor's busy schedule and also recognises that she is more likely to get a positive result if the doctor is not feeling too rushed.)

Dr Patel: *'Oh, hello Sarah, nice to hear from you. It's OK, I've got a few minutes before surgery. How can I help?'*

Sarah: *'Do you remember that we spoke a couple of weeks ago about Sean Roberts? I've visited him a couple of times since and I'm still concerned about his development. I'd really like him to have a full assessment at the Child Development Centre.'* (Sarah has decided that her main 'Broken Record' message is *'I want him to have a full assessment at the Child Development Centre.'*)

Dr Patel: *'I told you then that I didn't think it was anything to worry about. I'm more worried about his mother's drinking.'*

Sarah: *'Yes, his mother's drinking is a worry. Could we talk about that in a minute when we've sorted out Sean's assessment? He seems behind on several areas and I feel a full assessment at the Child Development Centre would be really helpful.'* (Sarah acknowledges that Sean's mother's drinking is a problem but does not allow herself to be sidetracked at this point. She puts the point to one side for discussion later.)

Dr Patel: *'Well, I haven't seen him that much you know; only when he had chicken pox last month. I didn't notice anything else wrong with him then, but his mother smelled of booze.'*

Sarah: *'That's my point really, it's nothing that hits you in the face, just a number of subtle things amiss. That's why it needs expert assessment such as the Child Development Centre can provide. I don't have the expertise and I know how busy you are.'* (Sarah ignores the reference to Sean's mother's drinking at present and tries to find areas of agreement with Dr Patel.)

Dr Patel: *'Well, I suppose I could but they have enormous waiting lists you know.'*

Sarah: *'Thanks so much for agreeing to do that. Yes, I do realise the waiting lists are awful but we've got to get started somewhere haven't we? Now about his mother's drinking . . .'*

By using the 'Broken Record' technique Sarah is able to get through Dr Patel's objections to reach her goal. If she continued to meet difficulty after repeating her message four or five times she could change to another message, probably one connected with the way in which the discussion itself is going.

Meta-level discussions

Discussing the discussion – known as meta-level talk – is often very helpful. This would involve phrases such as 'I'm worried that we seem to be having difficulty coming to an agreement,' or 'It seems as if we have opposing views here, is there some compromise we can reach?' This in itself could become the new 'Broken Record'.

By using the 'Broken Record' technique you can prevent the other person sidetracking or manipulating you with 'red herrings' and keep the focus of your discussion where you want it.

Exercise

Make a list of your needs which are not currently being met:

1 ....

2 ....

3 ....

4 ....

5 ....

6 ....

Taking each item in turn, plan how to request that your need be met using the guidelines discussed in this chapter:

- Step 1 – What exactly do you want?
- Step 2 – Who is the best person to ask?
- Step 3 – What are the effects of the request on the other person?
- Step 4 – When is the best time to ask?
- Step 5 – What is the best way to ask?

Chapter summary

Social workers constantly have to make requests for many resources for themselves and their clients. It is an integral part of the job.

There are several reasons why people hesitate to ask for what they want:

- They may have been taught as a child never to ask for what they want.
- As a child their requests may frequently have been ignored, leading to low expectations of satisfaction.
- They may see refusal as a rejection.
- They may fear being seen as 'needy' in some way.

People who *do* ask are more likely to have their needs met simply because others will know what they are.

It helps to have your request well thought out before you approach the other person. A five-step approach is:

- **Step 1 – Decide what you want.**
- **Step 2 – Decide who to ask.**
- **Step 3 – Consider the effects of the request on the other person.**
- **Step 4 – Decide when to ask.**
- **Step 5 – Decide how to ask.**

The 'Broken Record' technique is very helpful when the other person will not hear what you are saying. It can be used for making requests, saying 'No' – in fact any time when you have to be persistent to get your point across. To use the 'Broken Record' technique:

- **Step 1   Decide your goal.**
- **Step 2   State your case, including your 'Broken Record' statement.**
- **Step 3   Listen to what the other person has to say and decide if you will change your mind.**
- **Step 4   If you have not changed your mind, respond briefly to their comment and then repeat your 'Broken Record' statement.**
- **Step 5   Repeat steps 3 and 4 up to five times.**

7 Attending and chairing meetings

Meetings are an everyday part of the social worker's task – an essential part of making sure the client's needs are met. Social workers and social work managers attend many different types of meeting – family meetings, case conferences, allocation meetings and working parties to name but a few. Some are exclusive to participants from the worker's own organisation whilst others involve clients or workers from other agencies.

Sadly the truth is that a lot of meetings are overlong, boring and badly chaired. Being effective both at chairing and attending meetings helps your clients, reduces frustration and makes best use of your own and other people's time. If your weekly staff meeting is attended by eight people and runs over by half a hour each time, that's a total of half a day's work lost each week – and a lot of irritation to boot.

A common problem at meetings is that people grumble endlessly and fruitlessly or don't say they're unhappy but go away and complain in private afterwards. It can be very difficult to speak out against a group. A great deal of research has been done into group dynamics, and the power of the group should never be underestimated.

People whose view is not shared with the majority may keep quiet for a number of reasons:

- They fear the ridicule of the group for expressing different opinions.
- They feel lack of confidence for their own viewpoint, not having properly thought it through first.
- They believe they must be the only one with opposing views and that therefore they're outnumbered or just plain wrong in their belief (a particularly sad case this, as usually more than one person in the group shares their view but is keeping quiet).

Without assertive meeting skills you will feel increasingly powerless, your reputation will be damaged and your clients' needs will not be fully met.

81

These skills are rarely taught on social work courses and many people find it difficult, particularly when new in the job, to be assertive in meetings with other professionals who all seem very confident and determined to get their own way. The good news is that these skills, like any other, can be developed with preparation and practice.

Exercise

Think through the meetings you have attended in the last month. Identify the most and least effective meetings. Make a few notes on the questions below:

Most effective meeting

- What made the most effective meeting effective?
- What did the chairperson do to contribute towards the effectiveness?
- What did participants do to make the meeting effective?
- How would you evaluate your own participation in the meeting?

Least effective meeting

- What made the least effective meeting ineffective?
- What did the chairperson do to contribute towards the ineffectiveness?
- What did participants do to make the meeting ineffective?
- How would you evaluate your own participation in the meeting?

Your answers may have in part reflected the rights that individuals have in meetings, some of which are set out below.

Rights when chairing a meeting

Chairpersons have the right to:

- expect people to attend punctually
- control the meeting
- ensure that the business is worked through
- expect people to be prepared for the meeting
- ask for input from all relevant people
- expect people to stick to task
- finish on time

Responsibilities when chairing a meeting

Chairpersons have a responsibility to:

- send out agendas well in advance
- book the room and ensure that it is comfortable, at the right temperature and free from distractions
- be well prepared
- invite the correct people, perhaps asking people to only that part of the meeting which involves them
- control people who take up too much time
- encourage quiet people to have their say
- keep the group to task
- have suitable refreshments organised for participants
- take, or have someone else take, minutes or notes of the meeting
- circulate minutes of the meeting

Rights when attending a meeting

Participants in a meeting have rights that include:

- receiving an agenda and minutes of a previous meeting in advance
- having the meeting start and finish on time
- expecting others to be at the meeting on time
- being allowed to have their say
- being physically comfortable
- being protected from others who may attack verbally

Responsibilities when attending a meeting

Participants in a meeting have responsibilities that include:

- being punctual
- being well prepared
- keeping to task
- not interrupting others
- speaking 'through the chair' if that is normal procedure
- being succinct

Key assertive meeting skills

Step 1 – Know what you want

There is little chance of you working effectively in a meeting if you do not know what you want to get out of it. Do you want extra resources for a client? Do you want a child to remain at home? Do you want your duty system changed? Do you want the rota changed? Be clear and specific, but at the same time be aware of any areas of flexibility or negotiation.

Step 2 – Prepare

Thorough preparation is always important before a meeting, and especially so if you are intimidated by or impatient towards others. If you hesitate to speak out in meetings, it pays to read the minutes, agenda and any other relevant documents thoroughly, as it will increase your confidence. Plan exactly what you want to say and how you will say it. Consider what approach will be most likely to get the response you require. Who are the key decisionmakers? What angle will they be looking for? Do you need to adapt your approach to meet their preferred style or needs?

To overcome nerves, write down a few key words on a pad or index cards to prompt you. If there is a chairperson you can trust, consider asking him/her to make sure that you have an opportunity to have your say. If you have to make a presentation, rehearse it again and again until you feel completely confident. Make part of your rehearsal visualising yourself presenting really well – it will increase your chances of success enormously.

Step 3 – Know what others want

Of course, you can't be inside other people's heads, but try to make an educated guess about what they want from the meeting. Will they support any suggestions you make, or will they have different viewpoints? Will any negotiation be necessary? Chapter 12 on negotiation skills should help here.

Step 4 – Prepare solutions

To increase your confidence when making suggestions for change, have some ideas of your own to put forward. Base your ideas on what both you and the other person want to increase your chances of success. Be willing to listen to other people's suggestions though – they may be better than your own.

Step 5 – Find ways to reach agreement

If someone at the meeting continually blocks suggestions, ask questions such as, 'What would have to happen for us to ...?' This forces the person who is blocking into taking responsibility for finding a solution to their objection.

Exercise: Perfecting meeting skills

Think ahead to the next meeting you have which may present difficulties for you. Make a step by step plan of how you will handle the meeting. Now close your eyes and, as if watching a video, visualise yourself at the meeting. Keep 'changing the picture' until you are happy with how you perform at the meeting. Repeat this 'video' procedure several times before the meeting – your performance at the meeting will be considerably enhanced.

Case study – Linda fights for her client's rights

Linda's department had just brought in new regulations about who was entitled to community care help. One of her clients, Mrs Roberts, fell just outside the category and was due to have her help stopped. Linda felt very strongly that this would result in a serious deterioration in Mrs Roberts' condition. She decided to call a planning meeting quickly. She invited the case manager, her line manager and the district nurse. Mrs Robert's GP was unable to attend.

Using key assertive skills, Linda made the following plan:

- **Step 1 – Know what you want:** Linda wanted to try to meet Mrs Roberts' wish to stay in her own home.
- **Step 2 – Prepare:** Linda saw this as getting a really clear picture of Mrs Roberts' needs and the costs involved in meeting them.
- **Step 3 – Know what others want:** Linda knew that her line manager and the health professionals wanted life to be as simple as possible. They also needed to keep within their budgets.
- **Step 4 – Prepare solutions:** Linda intended to have clear plans including all costings ready for the meeting.
- **Step 5 – Find ways to reach agreement:** Linda felt convinced that by looking at the problem from the point of view of others involved she would have little difficulty persuading them to continue providing help to Mrs Roberts.

Linda knew that budgets were the greatest concern and planned accordingly. She worked out the cost of providing the existing level of care to Mrs Roberts, who, as well as having several physical problems, was just beginning to dement. She had once been found wandering the streets. Linda knew that Mrs Roberts wanted to stay at home and felt that this could be possible with increased help. In any case, places in residential homes were scarce and expensive. In fact she wanted to increase help by using a local church which could provide volunteers to call in daily to check Mrs Roberts. With the community care assistant calling three days a week and Meals on Wheels calling daily, she would be fairly well covered.

In preparing for the meeting, Linda made notes on:

- the cost of providing community care help to Mrs Roberts
- the cost of her own time in dealing with routine and crisis incidents with Mrs Roberts
- the cost of Meals on Wheels
- the cost of her time liaising with all involved

Against this, she set:

- the cost of her time in finding a residential home, getting Mrs Roberts installed and disposing of her home
- the cost of ongoing residential care, some of which the department would have to fund

Although Mrs Roberts needed quite a lot of help, the costs of keeping her at home were still significantly lower than residential care. Linda had all the figures neatly typed and had a copy ready for everyone at the meeting. She chaired the meeting herself and took control. She gathered up-to-date information from everyone about Mrs Roberts' condition and then clearly and succinctly outlined her plan. Her line manager agreed to keep providing help to Mrs Roberts although she fell outside the new strict criteria because he was able to justify this decision to his manager by providing the necessary figures.

Body language at meetings

Chapter 3 on body language explains how to sit assertively. When at a meeting you will look confident and assertive if you sit in this upright way with your lower arms resting lightly on the table – it looks very efficient and is good for your back. Have good eye contact with whoever is speaking, and show support for people by nodding your agreement. Make sure your tone is confident and firm when speaking – remember only 10 per cent of the message you give is with your actual words. Body language, tone and pitch account for the remainder, therefore congruence is essential or people will not believe what you say.

If you are finding it difficult to get a word in, try establishing eye contact with the person who is speaking – hopefully they will 'pass the floor' to you (the same trick works when trying to get served in a pub). Also consider using hand and arm movements to get attention, perhaps combined with sitting forward as if about to speak.

Assertive body language in meetings includes:

- **Posture** – upright, shoulders down
- **Head** – centred, not too high so that you are 'looking down your nose', firm but not rigid
- **Eyes** – good eye contact but avoiding staring
- **Face** – expression appropriate to what is being discussed
- **Arms/hands** – resting lightly on lap or table, open, not folded; hands relaxed, no clenched fists

Coping with interruptions

If people interrupt you when you are speaking, there are several steps you can take, and this is one occasion when you can learn a lot from politicians. Firstly, look at the person and say, 'Please just let me finish my point,' and continue speaking as if you hadn't been interrupted. Alternatively, you can simply raise your voice just a little and carry on speaking. If necessary raise a hand in a 'stay away' gesture (hand bent upwards at the wrist, palm towards the speaker).

Do try not to interrupt others, although if you have to do so, preface your remark with something like, 'I'll have to interrupt you there.'

Getting a response

It sometimes happens that you say something at a meeting and receive little response. If this happens to you, just ask for a response – 'What do others think?' 'Is that the way you see it?' – and then wait quietly for someone to speak. They will.

Stating opposing views

Inevitably you will occasionally have opposing views to someone else in the meeting. Keep calm and remember their rights to be treated with respect.

Before you launch into your views indicate your difference assertively by saying something like 'I have a different view on that' or 'I see that somewhat differently' or 'In my experience . . .' If possible, agree with something the other person has said: it will make them feel more comfortable and respected during potential disagreement – 'I agree with your main point; however, as I see it . . .' or 'That's a good way of looking at it, another way would be . . .' or 'That must be very annoying for you; on the other hand . . .' If possible, avoid using the word 'but' – it signals that the end of the sentence will contradict the beginning, and tends to block rapport.

Stopping 'overtalkers'

Almost every meeting has someone who hogs too much time. If you are chairing the meeting you could deal with this in a number of ways:

- by asking everyone to state their views and to keep it to a maximum of (say) two minutes
- by interrupting the overtalker with a comment such as, 'Thank you Jim, I'd like to stop you there because we haven't heard yet what Richard thinks.'
- in persistent cases, by speaking to the person outside the meeting and asking them to make briefer contributions in future

Dealing with people who digress

At every meeting, people wander off the subject. This is frustrating and time-wasting for everyone. Keeping in mind the topic under discussion, get people back to the point by saying something like: 'How does discussing caseload pressure help us decide how to plan the new layout of the office?' or 'I'm wondering how thinking about that now will help us reach a conclusion about this case.'

Chapter summary

Meetings are an everyday feature of life for all social workers and probation officers. Sadly, many are poorly chaired and timewasting.

People are often ill prepared when attending meetings – they fail to read minutes and agendas or to think through what they want to say at the meeting.

Peer group pressure is very powerful. For this reason it can be very difficult to go against the mood of the meeting. However, if your view differs from others, say so – the odds are that someone else is thinking the same thing but hasn't liked to say anything.

The chairperson at a meeting has rights and responsibilities. The rights include:

- expecting people to attend punctually
- controlling the meeting
- ensuring that the business is worked through
- expecting people to be prepared for the meeting
- asking for input from all relevant people
- expecting people to stick to task
- finishing on time

Participants at a meeting also have rights and responsibilities. Their rights include:

- receiving an agenda and minutes of a previous meeting in advance
- having the meeting start and finish on time
- expecting others to be at the meeting on time
- being allowed to have their say
- being physically comfortable
- being protected from others who may attack verbally

The five key steps to effective meetings are:

- **Step 1 – Know what you want.**
- **Step 2 – Prepare.**
- **Step 3 – Know what others want.**
- **Step 4 – Have suggestions as to how your goals could be reached.**
- **Step 5 – Find ways to reach agreement.**

Body language at meetings should be assertive – straight back, shoulders relaxed, head upright.

Other assertive meeting skills include:

- **dealing with interruptions**
- **interrupting others**
- **handling people who digress**

8 Giving feedback

Social work and probation staff are frequently in the unenviable position of having to say difficult things to clients whose whole sense of wellbeing may depend on their judgement. Just think about the areas of a client's life you can affect – these include their liberty, whether or not they keep their children or whether they have enough money to buy food. Difficult things social workers and probation staff say include things such as:

- 'No, the department won't give you money.'
- 'We don't have any housing of our own.'
- 'Because of your behaviour I will have to breach you.'
- 'If you don't do x, y, z, I will have to consider whether your child stays with you.'
- 'I am going to propose to the meeting that we take your child into care.'
- 'I'm sorry, the adoption panel turned you down.'
- 'I believe you have been sexually abusing your child.'
- 'I am not going to continue this interview because I believe you have been taking drugs.'

Honesty is essential

Few people enjoy saying hard things to others, and this is especially true for people who have chosen to go into the caring professions – on the whole they do care about people. Some workers wrap up messages in heavy cloaks of words to avoid hurting the client. When this happens the client can be left unsure about the nature or severity of the message. They have received a mixed message and can be justifiably angry when you later deliver the even more severe message that you'll take their child into care or breach them.

It can be harder still to criticise a colleague or boss. You have to work with them day in, day out and may like them; but avoiding difficult issues means that you just collect bad feelings instead ('stamps' – see pages 11–12) and one day explode and let them have it.

What stops us criticising others?

We can convince ourselves that we shouldn't criticise others for a number of reasons (see Table 8.1).

Table 8.1   Reasons we shouldn't criticise others

Reason	Faulty self-talk	Constructive self-talk
I might upset the person.	'Jane will be terribly hurt if I say that.'	'Jane might not like what I have to say but her chances of getting rehoused will improve if she acts on it.'
I've already said something.	'It's no good saying anything: nothing happened last time.'	'I will find another way to get this important message across.'
I'll get the blame.	'I won't say anything about Megan's poor financial position, she'll say I didn't help her enough.'	'I must explain that Megan's efforts so far aren't good enough and see what additional help she needs. I will refuse to take responsibility for her lack of action.'
She'll never speak to me again.	'I like my boss but she's really let me down. If I tell her how I feel she'll take offence.'	'I like my boss and will find a constructive way of letting her know how I feel. I will also let her know how much I value her.'

Reason	Faulty self-talk	Constructive self-talk
He'll lose his temper.	'If I tell him that I'm going to breach him he'll go crazy and might hit me.'	'I have to give him this difficult message. I will ask my line manager to be present in case the client becomes violent.'
I don't want to seem petty.	'I get so frustrated when Julie doesn't wash up the coffee mugs but it seems a little thing to go on about.'	'I have the right to expect others to take their share of the work. I will tell Julie how I feel and explore ways to make this work.'
I'm too angry to deal with this.	'I am so angry about this I'll kill her.'	'I'll wait till I've calmed down before tackling this situation. I'll work out the best way to say it and practise calming techniques.'

Exercise

Reflect back over the past week. Have there been times when you've either avoided giving criticism or done so clumsily? If so, why do you think this is the case? What steps can you take to avoid this happening again?

Tips for giving criticism

Criticise with empowerment in mind

It can be terribly tempting when someone has irritated you to let fly and criticise to make yourself feel better or to punish the other person. It is much more constructive (and less likely to lead to aggression) if you can criticise from a Nurturing Parent perspective (see Chapter 2).

Remember rights

You have the right to criticise other people as long as it is done constructively. Indeed, when it comes to clients you not only have the right, there is a professional expectation that you will do so in order to help the other person improve some aspect of their behaviour. Remember at all times that the other person has the right to be treated with respect.

Empathise with the other person

Before you begin to give criticism, put yourself in the other person's shoes. How will they feel receiving the criticism (not how *you* would feel if you were them – how would *they* feel)? This should help you to get an idea of how best to approach the problem.

Get your facts right

If you say to a client, 'You've been late for every meeting this month,' and this is not literally true you can be sure they'll come back with, 'No I haven't, I was on time two weeks ago.'

Be specific

With the right facts, you can be specific – this makes it easier for the other person to know how they need to change (see Table 8.2).

Table 8.2   Being specific

General criticism	Specific feedback
'You're always late for meetings.'	'During the last month you've been late for three out of four meetings.'
'You're failing as a mother.'	'Your children often go to school without breakfast, you have failed to collect them on time three times this week and they are often dirty.'
'You're too kind to your son [who has learning difficulties].'	'It would help your son to develop to his full potential if you allowed him to do x, y, z for himself.'

'Your attitude towards women leaves a lot to be desired.'	'I don't like the way you often say that women are just for cooking and sex.'
'Your supervision is hopeless.'	'In future during supervision I'd like us to cover x, y and z.'
'Your report is badly written.'	'Your report would read better if you changed it by adding x, y and z.'

Don't use universal words unless they are literally true

Universal words suggest that something is all-encompassing: 'Everyone...', 'No one...', 'Always...', 'Never...'

Choose your time

Whilst sometimes you have to give criticism when the behaviour is happening ('Don't put your hand near that machine, you'll lose a finger'), sometimes it is better to wait. If your colleague has been driving you crazy hogging the phone all the time for the past year, better to wait until you feel calm before you say anything. Criticising someone when the behaviour is *not* actually happening means that they don't have to lose so much face. Much better to find a time when both you and the other person are calm and receptive.

Choose your place

Always try to avoid criticising someone in front of others. No one likes receiving criticism, and to receive it publicly is doubly humiliating and sometimes blocks acceptance of the message as the person hastily fights to retain their dignity.

Try not to involve others

If you can own the problem as simply being your own, the other person may feel less exposed. If you say something like, 'Everyone thinks that...' or 'No one...', the person receiving the criticism is going to feel very uncomfortable with everyone else – 'Who said it? Why? Don't they like me? Are they all talking about me?' Sometimes, of course, you can't avoid involving others: you may have no personal knowledge of the situation, or perhaps another professional or a neighbour who wishes to remain anonymous has told you something.

Don't start your criticism with 'You ...'

Somehow criticisms started this way always sound more aggressive and blaming. Try starting with 'I' or another alternative: 'I've noticed that...' or 'In the past week...'

Don't guess at motives

We all tend to guess why people behave as they do – indeed social workers and probation officers are trained to do just this. However, the guess may be wrong, and telling the other person why you think they behave in a certain way can upset them because they may either feel uncomfortable that you seem to have read their mind or angry that you've misunderstood.

Criticise the behaviour, not the person

This subtle difference in delivering a message can be of vital importance. Imagine growing up with negative messages about yourself as a person rather than messages which tell you what is good and what is bad (see Table 8.3).

Table 8.3   Criticising the behaviour, not the person

Criticising the person	Criticising the behaviour
'You'll never amount to anything.'	'You didn't do very well in the exam.'
'You're a slob.'	'Your bedroom is untidy.'
'You're lazy.'	'I've asked you three times to wash up.'
'You're ugly.'	'That hairstyle doesn't flatter you.'
'You're a slut.'	'I'm not happy about you coming home so late.'
'You're a bad parent.'	'I'm unhappy that you shout at Tim so often.'

A four-step approach to criticism

This simple four-step approach will help you to sort out your thinking before you say something. It is often appropriate to involve the other person in the discussion rather than simply rattling through the whole dialogue.

Step 1 – Summarise the behaviour you're unhappy about

Remember the key is to criticise the behaviour, not the person:

- 'I've noticed three mistakes in your court report; they are . . .'
- 'Last week you were late collecting the children three times.'
- 'Carly looks unwell and her clothes are dirty.'

At the end of this stage it may be appropriate to ask the other person if they were aware of the problem. Sometimes a problem which is blatantly obvious to you is simply not an issue for the other person. Just saying something like 'Did you realise this?' can open up further discussion

Step 2 – Explain how you feel and why (if appropriate)

However, don't go overboard and tell the person you want to throttle them!

- 'I feel very angry about this because . . .'
- 'I feel irritated about this because . . .'
- 'I feel very disappointed with your behaviour because . . .'

Step 3 – State what you'd like to happen instead

Have in mind the steps you'd like the other person to take. Sometimes there is no choice; the person has to do x or y to avoid you taking action against them. Other times there is a choice, and people are much more likely to go along with decisions they've made themselves than those imposed on them by others.

- 'What do you think you could do about this . . . ?'
- 'How could this be resolved . . . ?'
- 'In future I need you to . . .'
- 'To avoid . . . you must . . .'

Step 4 – Consequences

Allowing for the fact that most people are more motivated by a carrot than a stick, try to identify something good that will be true for the other person if they change their behaviour:

- 'If you do this, little Jamie will be happier and play better.'
- 'If you do this, the electricity board won't disconnect you.'
- 'If you do this, I won't have to report to the court.'

Sometimes, however, you have to speak plainly about negative consequences:

- 'If you don't do this, I will report to the court.'
- 'If you don't do this, I have to issue your first verbal warning.'
- 'If you don't do this, I won't be able to recommend you for fostering.'

By the way, if you are angry it's easy to make negative consequences far too big – make sure the punishment fits the crime!

Case study – body odour problem

Let's look at this approach in action. Errol is a probation manager and has to deal with one of the most difficult situations a manager can face. Several members of his staff have complained about Ann, a probation assistant, who has a persistent body odour problem. Errol doesn't work in the same room as Ann but has noticed the problem once or twice. He waits until he has a free space in his diary and knows the same is true for Ann. He calls her into his room. He has worked out what he plans to say following the four-step approach. Because this is such a delicate subject, on this occasion he decides to use what would normally be step 2 first (see Table 8.4).

Table 8.4   Errol's four-step approach

Step 1	'Ann, thanks for coming in. I have to discuss something difficult with you. I feel really awkward raising this issue, but . . .'	Errol acts respectfully towards Ann. He realises that she is likely to feel embarrassed about what he has to say. He simply states the truth when he says he feels awkward.
Step 2	'I have noticed that you sometimes have a body odour problem. I'm not sure if you're aware of this.'	Errol does not involve others; because he has noticed the problem himself he does not need to say that others have complained to him. He tells her the problem in a straightforward way – there is no point in beating about the bush and giving a confused message. He checks if she has been aware of the problem.

Step 3	'Do you have any ideas how this could be resolved?'	By using neutral language ('How could this be resolved?' rather than 'What can you do about it?') Errol helps to depersonalise the issue. They explore options.
Step 4	'That's an excellent idea. I'm sure you'll feel more comfortable yourself that way.'	The positive consequence is likely to depend on how Ann responds.

Case study – the alcoholic

Barbara is working with an elderly man, Jim, who drinks heavily. He is in danger of being evicted from his flat because of non-payment of rent. He has several other problems including threatened disconnection of services and poor health. Barbara realises that he cannot deal with several issues at once and decides to speak to him simply about the most pressing matter. Jim has always denied that he drinks.

Step 1

Barbara: *'Jim, I need to speak to you about paying your rent. It hasn't been paid for six weeks.'*

Jim: *'Don't you worry your pretty little head about it, my dear.'*

Step 2

Barbara: *'I'm worried because your landlord is threatening to evict you if you don't pay regularly.'*

Jim: *'Oh, he's always saying that. I pay when I can, he knows that. I've got other things to spend my money on.'*

Step 3

Barbara: *'Jim, I'd like to ask the Benefits Agency to pay your rent direct. Would you agree to that?'*

Jim: *'What, me not deal with my own money? I'm my own man you know.'*

Step 3 (repeated)

Barbara: *'You'll still have control of the rest of your money, but I'd like to ask the Benefits Agency to pay your rent.'* (Barbara uses the 'Broken Record' technique here – see Chapter 6.)

Jim: *'I'm not sure about that. I'll have to give it some thought.'*

Step 4

Barbara: *'Just think about it Jim, you wouldn't have to worry about your rent any more. No more making sure it's there on time. Life would be much easier for you and you wouldn't have to worry about being out on the streets.'*

Jim: *'Well, I don't know, I suppose I could try it for a week or two. You'll sort it all out for me, won't you? My memory's not as good as it used to be.'*

Exercise

Think of a criticism you have to give someone in the near future. Write yourself a 'script' using the four-step format. If possible, ask a trusted colleague to role play the situation with you.

- Step 1 – Summarise the problem.
- Step 2 – Explain how you feel.
- Step 3 – Describe what you'd like to happen instead.
- Step 4 – Discuss the consequences – positive and (if necessary) negative.

Giving praise

Praise is an underdeveloped skill in this society. Many staff say that their managers don't praise them enough, and many social work clients feel the same about their social workers. As most people are motivated by praise, it is worth learning to praise even small improvements in a client's behaviour to encourage them to want to continue to receive this positive feedback. By building small steps to better behaviour in this way, huge changes can be accomplished gradually. Here are some tips for giving praise:

- **Use 'I' language** – own that *you* are pleased with the behaviour.
- **Praise the person and the behaviour**: 'I really like the way you dealt with Carly's tantrum then, Jane. You kept calm, didn't shout at her and

distracted her attention. Great!' 'I'm really pleased with the way you've managed your finances this week. You only ran out of money one day early. Well done.' 'You wrote that letter to the Housing Department really well: you said just the right thing.' 'You kept your temper really well during that meeting. I noticed you getting agitated but you controlled yourself well.'

- **Be specific, not general** – it helps the person to know exactly what they did right so they can do it again if they choose: 'I like your report – you explained how the family operate in clear and logical ways.' 'You spoke well at that meeting. You seemed to have all the facts at your fingertips and knew when to interject.' 'Your house is lovely and clean today. I like the way you've got everything looking so spacious.'
- **Tune in to the other person's value system** so that you can judge how to word praise to make it more meaningful: 'It was great the way you helped your wife then. It takes a man to handle something like that,' rather than 'You handled the kid's tantrum well.' 'When you put your mind to it you can plan ahead well. You're very intelligent,' rather than 'You planned that well.'

Accept that many people find praise difficult (workers as well as clients). Don't be put off by a throwaway response such as 'It was nothing' – for most people the praise is something to be treasured and remembered.

Chapter summary

People don't like to criticise for a number of reasons, including:

- fear of upsetting the other person
- having already said something and feeling that it's not worth the effort
- feeling you'll get the blame for whatever is wrong
- worrying the person won't speak to you again
- fearing an aggressive response
- worrying about appearing petty
- feeling too angry to deal with a situation calmly

When giving criticism:

- **Criticise with empowerment in mind,** rather than a wish to punish.
- Remember the other person's **right** to be treated with respect.
- **Empathise with the other person** – it will help you to say things calmly and in an undamaging way.

- **Get your facts right** before you speak – it will avoid the other person trying to deflect you with minor detail.
- **Don't use universal words unless they are literally true** – otherwise the other person will contradict you.
- **Choose your time** – unless it's essential to do so, criticise at a time when both you and the other person are in receptive mood.
- **Choose your place** – avoid criticising people in front of others.
- **Try not to involve others** – it makes it embarrassing for the other person to know that people have been discussing them.
- **Don't start your criticism with 'You ...'** – it tends to sound accusing.
- **Don't guess at motives** – you might be wrong.
- **Criticise the behaviour not the person** – this is less damaging for their self-esteem and less likely to invoke an aggressive response.

Use the four-step approach to giving criticism:

- **Step 1 – Summarise the behaviour you're unhappy about.**
- **Step 2 – Explain how you feel and why (if appropriate).**
- **Step 3 – State what you'd like to happen instead.**
- **Step 4 – Consequences.** First try a consequence which is positive for the person concerned. If that doesn't work, state a negative consequence. Never state a consequence you are not prepared to carry through.

When giving praise:

- Use 'I' language to let the person know that *you* are happy with the behaviour.
- Praise the person *and* the behaviour.
- Be specific, not general.
- Tune in to the other person's value system to make the praise as meaningful as possible.
- Accept that many people find praise difficult.

9 Learning from criticism

There are very few people who enjoy receiving criticism. Most of us have very unhappy memories from childhood of people criticising us in a hurtful way, and prefer to avoid repeating the experience. With practice, however, it is possible to not only cope well with criticism but also to learn from it.

So, how confident are you at handling criticism? Use the questionnaire below to check how sensitive you are. Put a mark on the scale to indicate your comfort level.

	Type of criticism	Comfort level (1 = very comfortable 10 = very uncomfortable)
1	During supervision your boss criticises your report writing.	1....2....3....4....5....6....7....8....9....10
2	A client calls you a name in the street.	1....2....3....4....5....6....7....8....9....10
3	A colleague moans at you for not washing up the coffee mugs.	1....2....3....4....5....6....7....8....9....10
4	Your partner tells you you have body odour.	1....2....3....4....5....6....7....8....9....10
5	Your boss comments on an embarrassing personal habit of yours.	1....2....3....4....5....6....7....8....9....10
6	Your boss unfairly accuses you of skiving.	1....2....3....4....5....6....7....8....9....10

7	Your secretary is sarcastic about your handwriting.	1....2....3....4....5....6....7....8....9....10
8	The receptionist tells you in public that she's fed up with you not signing in and out of the building.	1....2....3....4....5....6....7....8....9....10
9	Someone criticises your new jacket.	1....2....3....4....5....6....7....8....9....10
10	Someone makes a sexist remark about you.	1....2....3....4....5....6....7....8....9....10

It can be worth noting the type of criticism that most upsets you or how you are affected by criticism from different types of people. Are criticisms from clients OK, but those from colleagues more problematic? Are you comfortable about criticisms to do with your work but not about your appearance? Once you've noticed a pattern, you can begin to work at understanding your motivation and desensitising yourself to hurt.

Criticism can be good for you

Before we look at ways to handle criticism, it is worth noting that criticism is not all bad. Feedback can often be an invaluable aid to self-improvement. It tells us things about ourselves we may not have known. This is graphically demonstrated by a diagram called 'Johari's Window' (see Figure 9.1).

Things about you known to you alone	Things about you known to you and others
Things about you known to others but not to you	Things about you known to neither yourself nor others

Figure 9.1   The Johari Window

By being open to feedback from others you can extend your knowledge from the top two boxes to have a clearer idea of how others see you and eventually to have more insight into those 'hidden' areas in the bottom right hand box.

Criticism can be hurtful

Very, very few people enjoy being criticised – most of us experience feelings from slight discomfort to wanting the ground to open up when someone criticises us. If you have strong reactions to being criticised then it would be worth spending a few moments trying to recall how you were criticised as a child. Earlier in this book we saw that criticism of the whole person as opposed to criticism of the behaviour is especially damaging. If this has happened to you (and many parents criticise like this, not necessarily because they are wicked but because they know no other way) then it will probably have had two effects – it will have damaged your confidence, and you are likely to take criticism more to heart than others.

As we saw in Chapter 2, there are two personality types that are most affected by criticism in childhood: the Rebellious Child and Adapted Child aspects of the personality.

The worst thing that can happen to a young child is to be ignored. Babies who aren't touched and who receive no emotional nurturing can actually die, and are certainly likely to fail to thrive. A vacuum is the worst possible scenario for the development of both the physical and mental self. This being so, children will seek 'bad' attention if they can't get 'good' attention – in other words they'll be naughty. The parent then reinforces the 'bad' behaviour by giving attention to the child when it misbehaves (in the form of a smack or a telling off) and a vicious circle develops. Unless the parent changes tack and begins to reward good behaviour with praise and hugs, the child learns this dysfunctional way of behaving and continues in this way into adult life.

The growing child has to love its parents; it has to believe the parent is always right – there is no one else so important in its young world, so how could it be otherwise? If the parents continually criticise the child, at least it knows it exists; it's getting attention. Bad attention is definitely better than withdrawal of love in the small person's mind. If we use the Transactional Analysis model to explore this idea we see that the child is constantly receiving messages from the Critical Parent aspect of its caregiver(s) (see Figure 9.2). In response it is likely to become either overly passive (Adapted Child) or naughty (Rebellious Child).

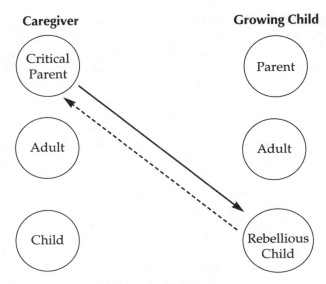

Figure 9.2   Bad attention – Rebellious Child

Another common reaction is for people to accept all criticism even if it's not true. We can develop this response reaction because we learn as a small child that if we don't fight back then love is not withdrawn; being good at least gains minimal attention (see Figure 9.3).

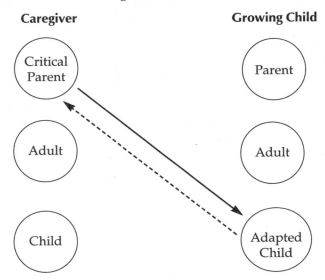

Figure 9.3   Accepting all criticism – Adapted Child

These messages are very powerful and become part of our unconscious motivators unless we uncover them in some way. Some children who are constantly criticised learn to protect themselves by building an invisible wall around themselves to stop painful messages getting through. This can translate in the adult to literally not hearing criticisms and behaving in a way that disregards others' feedback, or on the other hand, to being totally vulnerable to attack.

If it doesn't work, do something else!

With this early learning unchanged, we can continue to respond to criticism in the same old way indefinitely – with crumpling, ignoring or fighting back. Sometimes we develop what Anne Dickson in her book *The Right to be You* (1982) calls a 'crumple button' – an area or topic about which you are particularly sensitive because of early conditioning. It could be anything: your looks, your intelligence, your childcare or your accent. If you have one or more crumple buttons and someone talks about that area it is like someone has just pressed a button on your forehead and off you go responding in the same old way, even more than you would in other situations.

Even worse, we can hear criticism about our crumple button topics even when none was intended; perhaps the other person was making a perfectly innocent comment. Imagine your crumple button is about your intelligence; someone insults it and you go straight for the throat. Of course, they may not actually be insulting it – you just hear it that way. Perhaps they offer a suggestion on how to do something you already know how to do. Instead of hearing this as help you hear it as a criticism of your intelligence and ability.

A key skill in any criticism is to recognise the ego state which is 'hooked' by the criticism (and/or criticiser) and to learn to respond from a different ego state (see Table 9.1).

Table 9.1　Ego state responses to criticism

Criticism	Old response	New response
'That report you wrote was rubbish!'	'Yes, I know, I'll rewrite it immediately. Sorry.' (Adapted Child)	'What parts of the report aren't you happy with?' (Adult)
'You social workers are all the same, bloody waste of space!'	'How dare you say that after all I've done for you.' (Rebellious Child)	'What exactly are you unhappy about?' (Adult)

Generally, responding from the Adult state works well in this type of situation – it encompasses all the assertive skills and calm attitude you need to deal with and learn from the criticism.

Exercise

Think about the last few times you were criticised:

- What ego state did you respond from?
- Would another ego state response have been more helpful?
- What could you have said from that ego state?

Physical and psychological responses to criticism

With such strong early conditioning it is hardly surprising that our reactions are equally strong. People report a variety of physical responses to criticism, including:

- blushing
- feeling as if someone's punched you
- palpitations
- avoiding eye contact
- blood pounding in your ears
- shallow breathing
- stuttering
- holding your breath
- twitching

Likewise, there are many common psychological responses, including:

- feeling confused
- going blank
- wanting to hit back
- feeling hurt
- feeling like a child
- wanting the floor to swallow us up

With all this going on, it's hardly surprising that it's difficult to respond assertively!

Guidelines to responding to criticism assertively

- **Step 1 – Really listen to what the person is saying to you.** Do not automatically accept all criticisms or block any consideration of them.
- **Step 2 – Pause and give yourself time to think: 'Do I have to respond to this now?'**
- **Step 3 – When you respond, consider: 'Is this criticism true or untrue?'**

If true	If untrue
1 Admit it: 'Yes, you're right ...'	1 Deny it: 'No, that's not true ...'
2 Ask for more information if necessary, especially if the comment is very general.	2 Ask why they think it is true – there must be a misunderstanding.
3 Check out with others if appropriate.	3 If the person still thinks that there is a problem, use problem solving strategies.
4 Decide if you will change your behaviour.	

Step 1 – Listen to what is being said

This is easier said than done when your physical and psychological responses are throwing you into confusion and the blood is pounding so loudly in your ears that you can't hear a thing. By learning to control your immediate response to criticism (see the exercise on page 112) you can overcome these blocking responses. This would be a good opportunity to use a calming technique such as those described in Chapter 14.

Step 2 – Pause and give yourself time to think

We tend to believe that we should respond to criticism immediately, and this is sometimes true. However, there are times when you need time to reflect on what was said. If the person has hit you with something you haven't thought about, you may need time to consider whether the criticism is true or not.

If you do have to respond immediately, you can still buy a little thinking time by saying something like, 'Just give me a minute to think about that.' The brain works at least four times faster than the mouth, and simply saying that will give you time to be formulating a response, albeit at an unconscious level. Sometimes it will be possible to say, 'I'll need some time to think about that, let me get back to you about it.' This gives you time not only to consider whether the criticism is valid but also how to word your response.

Step 3 – Consider whether the criticism is true or untrue

If the criticism is clearly true or untrue, this may not be a problem. It's a little more difficult when there is a grain of truth in the criticism. For example, you are generally a punctual person but arrive 15 minutes late at a meeting. Your boss tells you off for being unpunctual. It's true that you were unpunctual on this occasion, but not that you are an unpunctual person. In this case your response could be something like, 'Yes, I am late today and I apologise for that, but usually I'm a very punctual person.'

If true, admit it

This can be very difficult for some people who simply can't allow themselves to show this much vulnerability. But it's really no good pretending that you haven't done something when you have (or vice versa) – you simply lose credibility with the other person.

Ask for more information if necessary

We have already seen that some criticisms are very general. In this case you don't receive enough information to judge whether or not it is appropriate for you to change your behaviour. You can gain information you can act on by asking questions such as:

- 'What exactly didn't you like?'
- 'How would you rather see it done?'
- 'What is wrong with it?'
- 'Which one exactly?'
- 'How does that cause a problem?'
- 'Can you explain exactly what you mean?'

If appropriate, check out with others

Imagine the criticiser says something like, 'Everyone thinks you speak too much at meetings' – you would be hard pressed to know whether or not this was really only the speaker's view. By asking other people you can get a better understanding of the situation.

Decide if you're going to change your behaviour

Remember, a criticism is generally just someone else's opinion. You will know if you want to change your behaviour. If someone criticises something that's important to you, you will be motivated to change. If they criticise something about which you care little, you may decide not to make changes.

If untrue, deny it

Simply say something like, 'That's not true' or 'That's not what happened.'

Ask the person why they believe it to be true

Unless the person is simply being awkward, the chances are that there's been a misunderstanding. By getting more details you can identify what the problem is.

Solve the problem

Now that you've worked out exactly what the problem is, you and the other person can use problem solving skills to resolve the situation.

Case study – the social work student

Tom was in his final year of social work training and undertaking a work placement in a psychiatric hospital. He and his practice teacher, Elizabeth, had a difficult but polite relationship. He found her rather hard to communicate with and wasn't pleased with the amount and type of work he'd been given. The workers in the department each had their own office and it was difficult to keep interrupting them for a chat or help. However, he had tried to be friendly to everyone and had often had coffee with the admin staff. During supervision, Elizabeth discussed with him the contents of the draft report she'd been writing for the college:

Elizabeth: *'Now Tom, this bit is about your relationship with colleagues within the department. I'm afraid I'm going to have to report that they've found you rather aloof and difficult to get to know.'*

Tom: (**Step 1** – Tom takes a deep breath to calm himself, he listens carefully to what she is saying and wonders if her comments really relate to *their* relationship. He puts himself into a positive frame of mind by talking to himself positively – 'I can handle this situation' – or by using one of the other techniques shown in Chapter 14.)

Elizabeth:	*'Did you realise this was a problem, Tom?'*
Tom:	(**Steps 2 and 3** – He decides he can handle this now. He believes the criticism to be untrue.) *'I'm amazed you should say that. I've got on well with people as far as I can tell, and I've never received that type of feedback before. I'm generally considered to be a friendly person.'*
Elizabeth:	*'Well, sometimes it is difficult to communicate with you.'*
Tom:	*'It would help if you could give me some examples. How many people have made these comments?'*
Elizabeth:	*'Well, um, someone made a remark to me a couple of weeks ago.'*
Tom:	*'So it's just one person. Is that how you find me?'*
Elizabeth:	*'I suppose it is – sometimes we don't seem on the same wavelength.'*
Tom:	*'We obviously need to talk about that in a minute, but can I have your assurance that you won't make such a general comment in my report?'*

Exercise

Try this exercise with a friend or colleague you can trust. The purpose of the exercise is to desensitise yourself in that awful first few seconds after you've been hit with a criticism.

Each write five criticisms about yourself which, if someone said them, would be true. Head your list 'True'. So, for example, if it's true that your desk is usually untidy, that your case recording is often out of date, that you spend too much time out in the smoking room, that you eat too many biscuits or whatever, write these down.

Now write down five things that are untrue for you. For example, if you are punctual write 'Unpunctual'; if you are energetic write 'Lazy'. Head this list 'Untrue'. Get your friend to do the same. Now swap lists.

Do brief role plays using the examples you've each provided. The point is simply to practise a very few sentences each to get past that initial uncomfortable feeling. A lot of short role plays can be very helpful here. And by heading your lists 'True' and 'Untrue' your partner can tell if you are denying a true criticism or accepting an untrue one.

Give each other constructive feedback. Tell each other a minimum of one thing you did well and one thing you could do differently – remember non-verbal as well as verbal communication.

Tips and hints for responding to criticism, sarcasm and put-downs

Remember that a criticism is not a personal rejection

If as a child you received criticism in a way which condemned you as a whole person, it can feel as if any criticism is a rejection of you rather than simply a comment on some part of your behaviour or ability.

Criticism is just someone else's opinion

Others may not agree with that opinion – you may decide that you don't either. An opinion is not a fact.

Use negative enquiry if you are unclear

Suppose someone has just made a sarcastic comment to you. Sarcasm and put-downs are particularly difficult to deal with because the other person often makes a throwaway remark (sometimes on the way out of the room). You can be left feeling unclear whether the comment is worth challenging, or even whether it was really a criticism or a joke. Likewise you may know that challenges bring responses such as 'Can't you take a joke?' or 'You misunderstood me.' Often we think of a brilliant, witty, cutting response a hour later – too late.

Actually, it's rarely too late to respond with a challenge. If necessary it can wait until the next time you speak to the person – 'About what you said last week...' Don't drop to their level, tempting though a cutting riposte may be – treat the sarcasm as a straight criticism (see Table 9.2).

Table 9.2　Responding to sarcasm

Sarcastic comment	Response
'I don't know about your hair like that – is it supposed to look like that or are you always in a hurry?'	'Don't you like my hairstyle?'
'This report is badly written. You're not nearly as intelligent as you look are you?'	'I'd rather you didn't comment on my intelligence in that way. What exactly don't you like about the report?'
'Here's Paul at last. Always gets to the pub after everyone's bought the drinks.'	'What exactly are you trying to say?'

Criticise the criticiser

If you constantly receive criticisms that you believe to be untrue, don't carry on responding to them, discuss the situation with the criticiser – in effect, criticise them for constantly criticising you. The section in Chapter 8 on giving criticism provides a format for this type of response.

Exercise

When we visualise something, it lays down the same pathways in the brain as if we'd actually done it. The more we visualise something, the more likely we are to change our behaviour and to be successful in achieving our desired state.

Imagine that you are with someone who you know criticises you. Picture yourself with that person in a typical criticising situation. See yourself as if you are on television. Now keep changing the picture until you are completely happy with the way you are responding. See, hear and feel the situation as fully as possible. Now imagine yourself behaving in the new way the next time the person actually criticises you. Does the new behaviour present you with any problems? If so, go back and alter the picture again until you are happy. Check again, and keep altering the picture until you are completely happy that the new behaviour will be of benefit to you.

Chapter summary

- **Criticism can be good for you** – It can help you to see yourself and your behaviour more clearly and enable you to decide on any changes you want to make.
- **Criticism can be hurtful** – Many people criticise in a hurtful way that does little other than dent the receiver's self-esteem. People who grew up with constant hurtful feedback often develop Rebellious Child or Adapted Child ego states as adults.
- **We tend to respond to criticism in the same old way** – By stopping and thinking about the situation we can respond from a different ego state and change the nature of the conversation.
- **Crumple buttons** are areas about which we are particularly sensitive. Sometimes we even imagine a criticism when none was intended simply because the person is discussing our crumple button area.
- **Physical and psychological responses** to criticism are often very powerful. They can make it more difficult for us to respond assertively.

An effective format for **responding to criticism** is:

- **Step 1 – Really listen to what the person is saying to you.** Do not automatically accept all criticisms or block any consideration of them.
- **Step 2 – Pause and give yourself time to think: 'Do I have to respond to this now?'**
- **Step 3 – When you respond, consider: 'Is this criticism true or untrue?'**

10 Saying 'No' and setting boundaries

Sadly, being able to say 'No' is one of the most essential skills for a social worker or probation officer. Unreasonable requests from clients and lack of time and resources mean that refusals are an everyday part of the job. Nevertheless, many workers feel uncomfortable having to say 'No'; after all, they are in the job to help people.

As with other behaviours, this difficulty often stems from childhood. We have seen earlier that as children we are often not given opportunities to use assertion and this is never more true than in saying 'No.' Children *are* expected to do what they're told and a refusal often brings unpleasant consequences. Little wonder then that this skill is a difficult one to acquire.

Childhood concerns are not the only reason why workers hesitate to say 'No.' Just look at some of the types of requests social workers and probation officers have to consider:

- housing
- money
- travel passes
- places in residential or day centres
- counselling
- extra work
- working late
- taking on particularly difficult work
- community care assistant time

In addition to the strictly professional requests people often find it difficult to say 'No' to requests such as:

- leaving present money for people they don't know or like
- sponsorships

117

- social events
- swapping duty or holidays
- giving their own children lifts or extra money

Consequences of refusal

Refusing these requests can bring anxiety in case others think we are incompetent, uncooperative, mean, unsociable or obstructive. Such worries may be realistic – if we are viewed negatively by line managers, for example, it could affect promotion prospects.

Frequently, though, fears about saying 'No' are unfounded; more a product of our imagination and uncomfortable feelings than reality. Nonetheless these fears affect our response to requests. If unable to say 'No' clearly, we can either give an unclear message or avoid saying 'No' altogether.

Workers often say that they find some requests easy to refuse and others very difficult. And just as some requests are more difficult than others, so some people are more difficult to refuse than others. Many people are brought up with a 'Respect your elders and betters' message and thus find it difficult to say 'No' to older people or those in authority. Sometimes it's difficult to say 'No' to clients you like, to people you find attractive or to children.

Exercise

Take a few moments to consider which people and what type of request you find most difficult to refuse. What makes these requests more difficult? It may help to spend a few minutes talking this over with a trusted colleague or friend.

Overcoming guilt

On assertion training courses participants frequently cite guilt as their main reason for failing to refuse a request. In some ways guilt is useful; it helps us to regulate our behaviour and stops us ignoring the rights of others. The negative side is that guilt, like worry, can be an overwhelming feeling driving all else from our minds. We know well that neither feeling is particularly helpful, but can feel powerless to take control of our minds.

Luckily we can learn to do just that – take control of our minds. Whenever guilt intrudes into your thoughts take this three-step approach:

Step 1 – Take whatever steps are necessary in the situation, whether it is saying 'No' or rectifying something you have done wrong.

Step 2 – **Learn what you can** from the situation.

Step 3 – **Think about something else!** This sounds easier than it is, of course, but it can be done. As those guilty feelings begin to crowd your mind acknowledge them, push them away and give yourself something to do that requires your concentration. Keep repeating this and your guilt feelings will gradually diminish.

Cost of always saying 'Yes'

Being unable to make appropriate refusals can be massively inconvenient to ourselves and sometimes to others. Consequences include being over-worked, taking on work beyond your ability, giving unclear messages, getting tired and raising clients' expectations unfairly.

Of course, by saying 'Yes' we aim to reduce our feelings of discomfort but this is often not the case. It is true that many people feel uneasy and guilty when they refuse a request, and naturally these are feelings we would rather avoid. However, saying 'Yes' against our better judgement simply brings a different range of unpleasant feelings. These may include resentment, anger and lowered self-esteem as we kick ourselves for not acting as we would wish.

When we consider these disadvantages it seems obvious that a clear 'No' is indeed the best policy for everyone involved. Saying 'No' appropriately does not make us horrible people; in fact, it can show others that we are trustworthy and consistent in approach. This does not mean that we go around saying 'No' indiscriminately. Of course it is the aim to help whenever possible, but circumstances inevitably mean that we cannot accede to every request.

Advantages of refusal

Being able to say 'No' has many advantages. These include:

- **Not taking on work your clients should be doing themselves.** Many people in the caring professions take on tasks that clients could do themselves, albeit with appropriate training. By continuing to treat clients in this way they become increasingly disempowered and reliant. Encouraging people to do everything they can for themselves is sound sense for everyone involved.
- **Having a realistic caseload.** It can be difficult to refuse to take on additional work when you know that your colleagues are all as busy as you. However, taking on work that you know you won't do properly and affecting your current caseload is not a realistic option and will damage your reputation.

- **Managing your time better.** Being able to say 'No' when necessary means that you will be able to deal better with interruptions and other inappropriate calls on your time.
- **Feeling good that you have made a balanced decision.** Not acting in a knee jerk fashion to requests is much better for your self-esteem.
- **Having a more constructive relationship with colleagues.** As colleagues realise that you can say 'Yes' or 'No' when necessary, they will realise that they don't have to look after you and can make requests of you with a clear conscience.

Setting boundaries

By letting other people know what your boundaries are you can often avoid having to say 'No' so often. Let people know if you:

- never give out money
- don't like going to the pub at lunchtime
- won't work late on Wednesdays
- don't want to be part of the Lottery group

or whatever. By doing this they'll stop asking you and you will save yourself a lot of time and emotional energy.

Tips and hints for saying 'No'

Recognise whether or not you want to accede to a request. Many people are so conditioned to saying 'Yes' that they don't even realise they wanted to say 'No' until it's too late. If this is true for you there is a simple way to make a more reasoned decision. Give yourself a second or two to listen to your body. If you don't want to go along with the suggestion you will probably have some uncomfortable body feelings such as a sinking feeling in your stomach. If you are happy to say 'Yes' you will probably feel quite comfortable and relaxed.

Remember that refusing a request is not rejecting the person. Unless someone has asked you for something very personal, such as a date, you are rarely rejecting the person. Keeping the two clearly separated in your mind helps you to keep the focus where it belongs.

Ask yourself if you have to reply now. Sometimes it is necessary to give a 'Yes' or 'No' immediately, but at other times you can ask for time to reach a decision. If you know that you want to say 'No' but can't bring yourself to say it immediately, this breathing space will allow you time to work out the best way to word your refusal. As with responding to criticism, if you do have to reply immediately give yourself a little time by saying something like 'Just give me a minute to think about that.'

Keep your body language assertive. Chapter 3 gives details of how to look assertive. The main point to keep in mind is that your verbal and non-verbal message must be congruent. Don't smile, have good eye contact, keep your head up and shoulders down.

Get the word 'No' out early in your reply. It is surprising how many people avoid saying the dreaded 'N' word altogether! Remember, people are not mind readers and if you give an unclear message they can be left confused as to what you actually mean. Worse, people who want to hear 'Yes' will take your lack of clarity as agreement.

If you want to, say how you feel about refusing the request. Not essential, but some people feel easier about refusing someone if they say something like 'I feel awkward saying this . . .'

Don't keep apologising. It's OK to say a simple 'I'm sorry I can't help you,' but once is the limit! Keep in mind that you are refusing a request; you haven't done anything wrong.

Keep your response short. Many people say far too much when refusing a request because of their uncomfortable feelings. Unfortunately, this often gives the other person a way in to try to persuade you to say 'Yes.' So if you say to a client 'I can't give you a lift because I have to call in to the office on the High Street before I go back to the office and then I have to get home promptly,' they could reply with 'That's OK. I can window shop in the High Street and I don't mind waiting whilst you're in the office or I could even walk from there!'

Give reasons, not excuses. It is strange that everyone sees through other people's excuses but somehow believe that no one will see through theirs. Of course, sometimes the reason is too harsh and one must keep the other person's rights in mind. If the reason is very damaging, for example 'No, I don't want to come for a drink with you because I think you're a crashing bore,' then simply avoid giving a reason.

Use the best words for the occasion. Remember how we used to be told as children 'There's no such word as can't.' Not literally true, of course, but often we do actually mean that we don't want to. There are a number of ways of saying 'No' that vary in intensity:

'No, I can't.'
'No, I'd rather not.'
'No, I'd prefer (to do something else).'
'No, definitely not.'
'No, I won't.'

Use a conversation closer. When you have finished stating your refusal don't let the conversation drift on. Use one of the following conversation closers to bring the discussion to an end:

- Offer an alternative such as 'I can't do that for you today, would Wednesday be any good?'
- Change the subject.
- Explore other actions the person making the request could take.
- End with a simple 'OK?'; said with the right tone it conveys that the conversation is at an end.

Exercise

Use the following checklist to help you identify times when you would like to say 'No'. Add other items that occur to you. When you have done this, work out how you will respond next time these requests are made of you.

Taking on extra work   ....

Working late   ....

Preparing a report at short notice   ....

Covering for a colleague   ....

Lending money to a client   ....

Lending money to a colleague   ....

Giving money to a charity you don't much like   ....

Sponsoring a colleague's child for a charity event   ....

Attending the team Christmas lunch ....

Giving someone a lift at an inconvenient time ....

Doing a home visit to someone who may be dangerous ....

Acting up for your boss ....

Being asked to sit on a committee ....

Seeing a client who has been drinking ....

....

....

....

....

Chapter summary

Saying 'No' is an essential skill for social workers and probation officers as they cannot possibly concede to every request made upon their time and resources.

Many workers hesitate to say 'No' because of:

- childhood conditioning
- lack of skills
- fear of possible consequences (even though these are often more imagined than real)

Saying 'No' can bring with it uncomfortable feelings, especially guilt. Guilt can be gradually overcome by:

1 **Taking whatever steps are necessary** in the situation.
2 **Learning what you can** from the situation.
3 **Thinking about something else!**

However, the cost of acceding to all requests can be high with increased workloads and pressure.

Advantages of refusal

Saying 'No' benefits the worker in many ways. These include:

- **Not taking on work your clients should be doing themselves,** and thus disempowering them.
- **Having a realistic caseload,** and a reduced stress level.
- **Managing your time better** by being able to control interruptions and other calls on your time.
- **Feeling good that you have made a balanced decision** and thus improving your self-esteem.
- **Having a more constructive relationship with colleagues.**

Tips and hints for saying 'No'

It is useful to set boundaries and let people know what those boundaries are. This should prevent you having to say 'No' so often.

- Recognise whether or not you want to accede to a request.
- Remember that refusing a request is not rejecting the person.
- Ask yourself if you have to reply now.
- Keep your body language assertive.
- Get the word 'No' out early in your reply.
- If you want to, say how you feel about refusing the request.
- Don't keep apologising.
- Keep your response short.
- Give reasons, not excuses.
- Use the best words for the occasion. There are a number of ways of saying 'No' that vary in intensity:
  - 'No, I can't.'
  - 'No, I'd rather not.'
  - 'No, I'd prefer (to do something else).'
  - 'No, definitely not.'
  - 'No, I won't.'
- Use a conversation closer:
  - Offer an alternative such as 'I can't do that for you today, would Wednesday be any good?'
  - Change the subject.
  - Explore other actions the person making the request could take.
  - End with a simple 'OK?'; said with the right tone it conveys that the conversation is at an end.

11 Handling aggression

It is unfortunately true that people working in the public sector are often at risk of aggression from their clients. By the sheer nature of their work, social workers and probation officers deal with society's most dangerous and mentally ill people, often in difficult and unsafe situations such as home visits. In the past few years:

- Isobel Schwarz, a hospital social worker, was killed in her office in 1984 by a client known to have a history of violence.
- Norma Morris, a social worker, was decapitated when making a home visit in 1986 for a mental health assessment.
- Louise Winspear, a solicitor's clerk, and Dennis Hull, a bailiff, were shot dead in 1987 serving an eviction order.
- Harry Collinson, a planning officer, was being filmed by TV cameras in 1991 trying to enforce an order in County Durham. He was shot dead in front of the cameras.
- Georgina Robinson, an occupational therapist in Torbay Hospital, was stabbed to death by a patient in 1993.
- Dr Gerald Flack was shot in 1993 by a man who felt Dr Flack had not done enough to save his mother's life. Dr Flack survived the shooting but was injured.

Whilst it is essential to acknowledge the risks of violence and aggression in a job, it is important to place these in a realistic context as fear can sometimes grow out of proportion to the actual risks. Luckily, most cases of aggression are not as extreme as these, but nevertheless they are frightening for the worker and sometimes have long-term effects on both physical and mental health. So why are people aggressive?

People rarely become aggressive in an instant unless they are mentally ill. Most people have a build-up period when perhaps a combination of circumstances leads to them feeling not in control of themselves or the situation – out of control in fact.

Case study

Jim, a 23-year-old man, has been out of prison for a week. The honeymoon period at home with his wife Julie and 2-year-old son Martin has quickly evaporated and real life has set in. The benefit cheque was due this morning but it didn't arrive. Julie is upset – there's no food in the house and there'll be nothing for Martin to eat. He's irritable enough as it is with some back teeth coming through, and he kept them up most of the night. She pressures Jim loud and long to do something about it. Tired of listening to her, Jim goes to the Benefit Office; he waits a long time to be seen and is met with an unsympathetic response. As he is leaving he remembers his meeting with his probation officer; he's got three minutes to get there and it's ten minutes' hard walk away. At least, he thinks, he can get enough money from them to tide him over.

Arriving at the Probation Office, Jim is met with the news that his probation officer is not yet out of a meeting and he'll have to wait 15 minutes. What sort of a reception do you think the probation officer is going to get when they eventually meet? How would you feel in Jim's position?

Causes of aggression

Threat to basic human needs

Jim's case is a good example of the fact that we all have what are seen as essential needs. Think for a minute of the basic needs we all have. These include:

- good health
- freedom
- safety
- shelter
- food and drink
- relationships
- mobility
- self-esteem

Social workers and probation staff between them can seriously affect clients' access to all these basic human needs. A threat to any of them is not to be taken lightly; threats to several at once are even more serious.

Frustration

Trying unsuccessfully to make your needs understood can lead to strong reactions such as fear and frustration. Frustration often builds up until people have an outburst – a tantrum if you like. Even professional people have tantrums. They may not be the same as a 2-year-old lying on the floor in the supermarket screaming and kicking, but they're simply the grown-up version of the same emotion. Have you ever slammed a drawer when it won't open or shut properly, shouted at a shopworker who gives you bad service, thrown down the screwdriver across the room when the screw just won't go in straight?

Many clients have valid frustrations:

- a giro not arriving when it should
- waiting ages to see a worker
- being pushed around from one agency to another
- their childcare ability being doubted
- being told to do things they don't want to do
- not having their property repaired by the Housing Department
- being given incorrect advice by a worker
- not feeling listened to
- being treated with disrespect by a worker

To workers, these events may be an everyday occurrence – we see people with similar problems day in, day out. It's quite different for the client though – these frustrations affect something of real importance in their lives, from their ability to feed their children to being able to hold their head up and feel good about themselves. Putting ourselves in the other person's shoes, being empathetic, can often lead us to act quite differently towards a frustrated client.

Fear

People can be fearful about all sorts of things. Vida Pearson in *The Causes of Aggression* (1992) says that fear arises because people register a threat to themselves of personal damage, injury or discomfort; losing or not gaining the satisfaction of a basic human need, or losing or not gaining a privilege. Social workers, probation officers and other care workers have the power to affect all of these:

- Prison staff can ignore a prisoner's fear of violence from other prisoners.
- Hostel staff can ignore a resident's fear of violence from other residents.

- Social workers and probation staff can refuse people money which they need to meet several essential needs.
- Social workers, probation and housing staff affect people's ability to have a roof over their head.
- Social workers and probation staff can affect people's relationships in many ways – not least by removing a child into care.
- Probation staff can affect their clients' chance of liberty.

Exercise

Think for a minute how you would react if you thought one of the essential needs was going to be taken away from you.

Now imagine yourself as a client, with few verbal resources and even fewer financial ones, trying to get what you need from a professional.

Which of these basic human rights would you be willing to fight for?

Esteem needs

Don't underestimate the 'softest' of these – self-esteem. Whilst as a worker it may be easy to tell that someone is worried about losing their home or not having enough money to feed their children, feared loss of self-esteem is often well disguised. Take for example a situation where the client is required to read or write something during an interview (or even fears they may be asked to do so) and is in fact illiterate. Many people try desperately to cover up their illiteracy. One tactic is to get angry and rubbish the whole interview, leaving the worker completely confused as to what the aggression was about.

People also become fearful when they can't understand what's being said to them. Think for a moment of the meetings and courses you've attended. There have undoubtedly been times when you failed to understand something but said nothing for fear of looking stupid. This is a very common reaction.

Clients are often faced with rules and regulations which are difficult to understand, and workers sometimes use long words, initials and jargon clients don't know. The client then feels foolish asking for things to be repeated, and again covers up with anger.

Furthermore, clients are often asked to attend meetings – something which may be completely alien to them. During the meeting they may hear difficult things said about themselves and lack skills to handle the situation effectively.

Injustice

The care system is not always just: regulations vary from borough to shire; individuals interpret regulations differently; cuts are an ever-present fact of life. Sometimes workers are prejudiced or just plain exhausted. Sometimes the rules themselves seem not to offer justice to everyone. Injustice is suffered by many groups of clients on the basis of their skin colour, religion, race, gender, education level and class.

Black people can be treated with injustice in several ways:

- They may face a prejudiced worker.
- Their ethnic needs may not be understood or catered for (for example, dietary needs in a day centre).
- They receive harsher sentences in court than white people.
- Assumptions are made about them on the basis of their colour.
- Differences in body language may be misinterpreted.

Injustice based on gender includes:

- assuming that a woman will take care of an elderly relative, whilst having no such expectations about her brother
- giving a man looking after an elderly woman more help than that offered to a woman in a similar position
- assuming that a man is less capable than his partner of looking after their children
- pushing the woman more quickly up the tariff scale by recommending that she receive a probation sentence to give her 'help' when the worker would have recommended a man receive a conditional discharge
- assuming that women committing 'men's crimes' are in some way worse than men, and mad, bad or sad

Injustice based on class includes:

- not using language with which the client feels comfortable
- making assumptions about the client's needs
- making assumptions about the client's tastes and preferences
- having lower behavioural expectations of some clients

Are you triggering aggression?

So far in this chapter we have concentrated on the fear, frustration and injustice done to clients. Of course it is true to say that workers also have the same emotions and often the same reactions, despite training to provide a professional approach.

Case study – Maya

Maya is a black 26-year-old generic social worker working in an Inner London borough. She was late arriving at work this morning because her child was ill and it was touch and go whether the childminder would take him for the day. Feeling rushed and unprepared, she entered a planning meeting where her boss contradicted her views several times. After the meeting, with just fifteen minutes before she had to leave for a client's house, she tried to make a few important phone calls. She waited ten minutes before a phone became free, and then couldn't find anyone she needed in. On the way to the client's house she got stuck in traffic and was ten minutes late. Arriving at the estate, she was dismayed to find that there were no parking spaces where she could keep an eye on the car (the estate was notorious for vehicle damage). She knocked on the client's door and was met not only by the client but also by a huge, ferocious-looking dog. The client looked surprised to see her: 'Who are you?' he demanded gruffly, 'I'm expecting the bloody social worker.' It was clear that because she was black and young he couldn't accept that she was in a professional role.

It would be entirely possible that instead of handling this situation calmly, Maya could trigger a violent incident by her irritation (caused by the preceding events) showing in her voice and body language.

Exercise

Have you ever been aware of overreacting to a situation because of something that was actually nothing to do with what was going on at the time? If so, try to work out what triggered the strong reaction you felt. Did the other person remind you of someone you don't/didn't like? Did you feel embarrassed or in some way inadequate in the situation, and so 'cover up' your feelings with aggression?

Your strong reaction could escalate an already tense situation or even trigger one in the first place. Learn to recognise your own early warning symptoms of rising anger so that you can calm yourself before you respond.

Giving aggressive messages

As we have seen, social workers and probation staff may trigger aggression by being affected by preceding events or by reacting inappropriately to situations as they arise. This can be on an obvious level such as not taking an elderly, frail person to the bathroom quickly enough, thus provoking an outburst. But it could be more subtle: an unconsciously clenched fist or jaw when the client is speaking. It helps to recognise your early internal signs of anger arousal so that you can take steps to overcome them. Such signs include:

- shoulders raised
- tight feeling in the head
- twitching
- tight feeling in the pit of your stomach
- changes in breathing
- feeling hot

By learning to recognise your own early warning signs you can take preventative action (see Chapter 14) to ensure that you do not inadvertently make matters worse. If you are not sure what your early warning signs are, you have two courses of action. Others who know you well will be able to tell you your first visible signs (if they dare!). Better still though, next time you are in a stressful situation consciously take note of your bodily sensations. Check these out for a few such situations until you can begin to change your reactions almost without thinking. Remember that for most behaviour change twenty to thirty repetitions of the new behaviour is all it takes to become second nature.

Recognising early warning signs in others

When you learn to recognise your own early warning symptoms you will have the advantage of being able to spot them *before* they become visible to others. Sadly, you won't have the luxury of being able to spot approaching aggression in others until it becomes visible.

Non-verbal signs

External signs of aggression are numerous and unfortunately often appear contradictory. However, by considering the context of the situation and topic of discussion and by using empathy skills you should be able to detect these non-verbal signs with a little practice:

- clenched jaw
- throbbing vein in neck or temple
- jutting jaw

- clenched fist (sometimes hidden under armpit)
- 'eyeballing'
- sudden change in posture
- standing when previously sitting
- leaning forward
- raised fist
- banging fist on desk or table
- stamping foot
- tapping fingers
- flushed neck and/or face
- frown
- fluttering eyelids
- intense smoking
- twitching
- tutting
- looking straight through you
- heavy breathing
- sweating
- sudden movement
- skin tone changes
- frozen smile

Verbal signs

Think of the most sinister characters on film – they don't all act like Arnold Schwarzenegger, in fact they are often very quietly threatening: more Bob Hoskins than Arnie. It sometimes takes a while for someone to say something aggressive; it's more the way they say what they say rather than the actual words. It pays to consciously listen for these signs, which include:

- speaking slowly
- mimicking
- sarcasm
- change in tone
- mumbling
- shouting
- swearing
- tutting
- depersonalising you
- stuttering

All of these verbal and non-verbal signs are part of what's called 'non-verbal leakage' (see Chapter 3). Non-verbal leakage occurs when the person is

trying to disguise an emotion but it 'leaks' through in some way. The leakage itself won't necessarily tell you what they're unhappy about, but again by considering the context you can probably tell whether the person is becoming agitated or if there's more likely to be a perfectly innocent explanation for the leakage.

Responding to aggression

You already have skills at coping with aggression. If you have worked through this book you will have added to your existing ability a very useful set of skills in dealing with aggressive people. As well as using your body language effectively, you will have a range of rapport skills, be able to give criticism constructively, receive criticism calmly and say difficult things assertively. These skills will take you through a whole array of tricky situations.

'Fogging'

Sometimes aggressive people make provocative comments which are best ignored. If this is the case you can use the fogging technique – so called because it doesn't give the other person something to focus on. To use this technique, simply agree with something the person says while ignoring those bits you don't agree with, for example:

- 'You may be right.'
- 'I can see you feel strongly about that.'
- 'I can see that's annoying for you.'
- 'That's one way of looking at it.'

Be careful with this technique: if there's a trace of sarcasm in your voice it can sound as if you are being disrespectful. However, used with integrity to acknowledge the other person's feelings while keeping control of the situation, it can be very valuable.

Tone of voice

There are two basic ways to use your voice (as opposed to your words) when dealing with an aggressive person. The first is to keep your voice calm and low. Margaret Thatcher used this technique very effectively with many media interviewers. This works very well for some people. However, other people are more wound up by someone keeping calm – they think the person is not taking them seriously. A useful alternative in this case would be to match the person's urgency of tone. This does not mean that you get angry back, you simply speak louder than normal to show that you are on their wavelength. Chapter 4 on rapport skills goes into more detail about how people feel comfortable with others who seem like themselves.

Consider this conversation:

Angry client (John):	*'How many times have I got to say this. My giro didn't arrive this morning and I've got precisely 50p to my name. You tell me how I can feed three kids till tomorrow on that. There's no food in the house.'*
Worker:	*'Yes, I can imagine that's a worry for you but I'm afraid we're not in a position to give out money.'*
John:	*'Well then, you can have my kids for the night. I'm sick of this – you lot never listen. I try really hard to keep the family together after that so-and-so of a wife goes off and leaves us and what help do I get?'*
Worker:	*'I can see it must feel like that sometimes, and you've been doing a great job with your kids, but we do give you quite a lot of help in other ways. Shall we see if there's any other agency that can help?'*

Try reading this conversation out loud both ways, first with the worker being quiet and calm, and then speaking with a raised (not angry) voice and with some urgency. Either will work, although the skill is in judging which to use with which person. There is no golden rule, unfortunately – it's best to try using whichever of these two styles feels natural to you, and if this doesn't work, quickly change to the other.

Dealing with confrontations

So far we have looked at several aspects of responding to aggression, now we'll look at a step by step flowchart for dealing with the confrontation itself. These steps should be taken as a guide only, and should be adapted as necessary. It may be necessary to repeat any step several times, and of course, if the aggression stops there will be no need to continue through to the end of the suggested format. Remember any of the responses in Table 11.1 could be said in the quiet and calm way or the slightly louder, firmer way.

Table 11.1   Dealing with confrontation

What to do	Hints	What to say (example)
Step 1 – Stop, listen to the angry person, use active listening skills, let them run out of steam before attempting to seriously join the conversation.	Keep calm, have good inner dialogue, concentrate on listening to the person and observing body language.	(to yourself) 'I can handle this' – but if in any doubt get out immediately: do not put yourself in danger of physical attack.
Step 2 – Respond assertively, check if you have understood correctly (angry people are often unclear). This allows the other person to feel heard or correct you.	Use fogging technique if necessary. Keep your integrity.	'Can I just be clear I've got this right? What you're upset about is . . .'
Step 3 – Point out any contradictory comments the client has made.	Only do this if you feel it safe to do so. If you think they'll become more angry, go with whichever interpretation you feel correct, and check your understanding.	'On the one hand you're saying . . . and on the other . . . I'm not clear which one is of most concern to you.'
Step 4 – If aggression continues, repeat steps 1–3.	Continue to assess your level of safety. Do not leave yourself open to physical attack.	'It seems that you're saying . . .'
Step 5 – If the aggression continues, let the client know you are unhappy about the situation.	Keep calm, make sure your body language is congruent. Don't threaten consequences you won't carry through. Use the 'Broken Record' technique if appropriate. Check agency policy on terminating interviews or hanging up on a client.	'I'd really like to help you sort this out but I can't while you're shouting at me. Let's sit down and discuss this quietly. Otherwise I'll have to end this conversation now.' *Continued overleaf*

What to do	Hints	What to say (example)
Step 6 – End the discussion, or start discussing the discussion itself.	Discussing the discussion is often a useful way to take things forward. You do not discuss what the discussion is about, but the process itself.	'I have tried several times to sort this out with you. Is there some way we can resolve this matter?'

This approach combines several assertiveness skills – effective listening, empathy, summarising, 'Broken Record', fogging and rapport building.

Additional tips and hints

Jointly own the problem

Talk in terms of 'we' rather than 'I', adopting a joint problem solving approach to the situation. Not all solutions can be jointly owned, of course – sometimes you just have to tell the client what to do to avoid a child being taken into care, being breached, etc. When using 'we' make sure that you don't sound patronising or you could inflame the situation.

Make the limits of your responsibility clear

Often clients aren't clear about whether you or the organisation is responsible for an unwelcome decision. So instead of saying 'I can't...', say 'The rules are...' or 'Social Services doesn't allow...' This stops the client blaming you and shifts responsibility to the appropriate place.

Use your listening skills

It's easy, especially if you are fearful of your safety, to listen to superficial messages only. Try to listen to the message behind the words – it may help you calm down the situation more quickly.

Try different approaches

When you feel aggression is approaching, you could try the methods already suggested. Alternatively, you could try humour, but *not* at the client's expense – joke about something over which neither of you has control. Offering to make a cup of tea or coffee, or fetching a biscuit, can sometimes take the heat out of the situation and disarm the client.

Move!

If you are aware that your joint body language is confrontational (e.g. facing each other, leaning forward) then move yourself slightly so that your body is facing slightly away. You will still be able to look at the other person, but will appear less threatening.

Personal safety during home visits

Home visits present a very real danger for the social worker or probation officer. You are on the client's own territory (unfamiliar to you) with possibly no means of getting help. There are several aspects of home visits to consider.

Getting there

Plan your journey in advance so that you don't waste time, but more importantly don't drive round potentially dangerous areas unnecessarily. If you are going to an unfamiliar address on an estate get detailed instructions before you set out, and don't spend time driving slowly or parking some way off and having to walk the rest.

Don't have anything in the back of your car that advertises the work you do – keep briefcases, case files, etc. out of sight.

Park as close as you can to the client's property, and reverse into the parking space so that you can make a quick getaway if necessary.

Walk confidently as if you know where you are going, even if you don't. Don't look like a social worker! Don't look like a victim either.

Carry a personal safety alarm, and don't put it in your briefcase or bag. Keep it somewhere where you can get to it easily. No one's going to hold off their attack until you find it.

On the doorstep

Look around before you go into the house/flat. Is there any potential danger? Ask for any dogs to be put into another room. Ask who is at home – if there are extra people present consider rearranging the appointment. Check the way the door locks so that if you have to make a hasty exit you won't feel so flustered.

Inside

Look around and note exits. See if there are any potential weapons the person could use against you. Heavy ashtrays, ornaments, pokers, dining chairs can all be used in this way. If you feel at all threatened, sit near the door, preferably on an upright chair – they're easier to get out of. Keep your bag/briefcase near you and your car keys close to hand so that you can pick them up quickly as you leave.

Leaving

If possible, let the client go to the door first – it stops them grabbing you from behind. If you are really in danger, leave your things behind and just get out fast. If you think you are visiting a dangerous client, consider whether you should take anything with you that could identify your personal details – the last thing you want is the client arriving on your doorstep or making nuisance phone calls.

After a violent incident

Departments and managers vary in their response to workers after a violent incident. Hopefully your manager will be sensitive to your needs, but it may be that you need to be assertive to get your needs met at this difficult time.

People respond differently following an aggressive incident; some seem to sail through with no damaging effects, others range from needing time for a cup of coffee to needing counselling. If you are upset by an incident, you will need time to calm down. It can take up to ninety minutes for your adrenaline levels to return to normal, and during this time it will be difficult for you to concentrate on anything. During this period you may experience extreme moods or even mood swings – be assured that this is not unusual. Many people need to retell the story again and again as a way of working through their feelings; others prefer not to discuss it. Some people need time off work. If this should happen to you, tell your manager. He or she may well be able to arrange for you to have counselling, and some authorities have a scheme to cover the cost of this for their staff.

Chapter summary

There are many causes of aggression. These include:

- **Threat to basic human needs** – health, freedom, safety, shelter, food and drink, relationships, mobility, self-esteem.

- **Frustration** – many clients are frustrated when events don't go according to plan, often through no fault of their own.
- **Fear** – clients may fear personal injury from others, or that the worker will affect their life in some unacceptable way.
- **Esteem needs** – clients can often feel inadequate around professional people who have skills and knowledge they lack.
- **Injustice** – many clients face injustice from both individual workers and the agencies they work for. This injustice is sometimes based on race or gender.

Sometimes workers trigger aggression by thoughtless behaviour or by unconsciously showing through their voice and body language that they are feeling aggressive themselves.

Be aware of your own early warning signals. To avoid giving threatening non-verbal messages to the client learn to recognise your own early warning signals that you are becoming annoyed. This enables you to take avoiding action for yourself.

Be aware of your client's early warning signals. Learn to recognise the very first signs of aggression in others so that you can get away or take steps to calm the situation.

The fogging technique can be useful when dealing with aggressive people. Simply agree with some part of what the person is saying to avoid getting into an argument. If there is nothing else to agree with, you can acknowledge their feelings.

When talking to an aggressive person:

- **Jointly own the problem.**
- **Make the limits of your responsibility clear.**
- **Use your listening skills.**
- **Try different approaches.**
- **Move!** Change position if you realise that you and the client are locked into aggressively matched body language.

Personal safety and home visits:

- **Getting there** – Plan your journey in advance, don't advertise that you are a probation officer or social worker, carry a personal safety alarm, park close to the client's property, back into the parking space to enable a quick getaway.
- **On the doorstep** – Look around for potential danger, ask for dogs to be shut away, consider leaving if additional people are present, check locks.

- **Inside** – Note exits and potential weapons, keep your keys near at hand.
- **Leaving** – Let the client go to the door first.

After a violent incident: People respond differently following an aggressive incident – it is important to make your needs known to your line manager and others.

12 Negotiation skills

Negotiation is an everyday part of the social work task. Social workers negotiate for resources, for caseloads, for duty swaps, for decisions in planning meetings and a whole range of other things. Many of the skills already covered in this book are invaluable in negotiation. Having the ability to keep calm, to empathise, to separate people from issues, to use rapport skills will all enhance your chances of reaching your desired outcome. The two key factors to success are preparation and confidence – get these right and everything else will follow naturally.

To help you in your preparation, try this exercise.

Exercise

Work quickly through the questionnaire on page 142 considering your confidence level in relation to each item. Put a tick in one of the three boxes for each item. For example, if you can quickly understand core issues, put a tick in the 'confident' box. This questionnaire will help you identify your strengths and development areas for future negotiations.

Item	Confident	So-so	Poor
1 Quickly understand core issues			
2 Able to identify clear goals			
3 Keep my mind on the goal			
4 Understand negotiating norms in other cultures			
5 Listen effectively			
6 Able to know what preparation to do before a negotiation			
7 Can develop a range of strategies			
8 Read body language signals correctly			
9 Know how to time interventions			
10 Want to win for myself or my client			
11 Assess people effectively			
12 Cope with stress in negotiations well			
13 Can separate facts from assumptions			
14 Stay within bounds of what is possible			
15 Able to understand the other person's pressures and viewpoint			
16 Don't get self or others cornered			

You may also find it helpful to consider how your family handle(d) conflict. When in this type of situation, were family members:

● confronted assertively?

- ignored?
- denied a right to speak?
- listened to respectfully?
- met with violence?
- blamed?

Your negotiation style may still be based on that which you experienced as a child, so it is well worth considering this possibility. How does your previous life experience affect your confidence level in negotiations? How does it affect what you say and do? How does it affect the way in which you view your opposite number? Does it lead to you making assumptions about the other person which may be based more on what you think than on reality?

Source: Adapted from Schapiro (1993).

What goes wrong in negotiations

The questionnaire above suggests things that commonly go wrong during negotiations. These include:

- lack of preparation
- no game plan
- insufficient facts
- inflexible approach
- attacking the person rather than the issue
- using the wrong negotiating tactic
- lack of confidence
- having no clear goal or bottom line
- unrealistic expectations
- cultural misunderstandings
- having hidden agendas
- failing to read the other person's body language

Prepare, prepare and prepare again

Preparation is one of the essential keys to success in negotiation. How much preparation do most social workers undertake when in reality they're rushing from client to phone call to meeting? Probably nothing like as much as their clients (or they) deserve.

In any negotiation you have to consider:

- the personality of the players in the game

- the outcome you want
- the outcome the other side wants
- what you will be willing to concede
- what you will be willing to accept
- your bottom line
- what you think they will be willing to concede
- what you think they will be willing to accept
- what you think their bottom line is

Exercise

Think ahead to your next negotiation and, using the points above, make a step by step plan to develop your approach.

Goal setting

All this naturally assumes that you know what you want – that you have a goal in mind. It may be that there is no flexibility, that you will accept no less or more than a certain outcome. Alternatively, you may be open to one of several possibilities. It is worth repeating that the important thing is to know what you want and what your bottom line is. The SMART acronym is helpful when you are formulating your goals:

- **Sensible** – Goals should be realistic – it's no good expecting an unruly teenager to become a model citizen overnight.
- **Measurable** – You should be able to measure whether or not the goal has been achieved – 'I need to be sure that you've collected your child from school *every day*,' not simply, 'You must collect your child from school.'
- **Achievable** – It's no good setting a goal which your client or colleague can't possibly reach.
- **Reasonable** – Goals must be rational.
- **Time-bound** – There should be a time limit to the goal to ensure that assessment is not left too long – 'For the next two weeks you must collect your child from school every day. We'll meet then to discuss progress.'

Exercise

Write yourself a goal for your next negotiation. It doesn't have to be anything big – asking a colleague, yet again, to wash up the coffee mugs; trying to persuade your boss to let you have that special day off; getting your own phone installed instead of having to share one. Make sure that your goal as written meets the SMART requirements.

Now imagine yourself as the person you are going to negotiate with, and try to write down their goals.

Your negotiating power base

Even though you may feel you have little power in terms of budget decisions and some other areas of authority, there are several types of power you do have. Those identified by Nichole Schapiro in *Negotiating For Your Life* (1993) include:

- **positional power** – your power as a social worker and as a representative of your organisation
- **expert power** – your power as the social worker involved in the situation, with all your training and experience
- **perceived power** – how other people see you
- **personality power** – the power you exert simply by the use of your personality: charisma
- **connection power** – the power you have from your knowledge of networks and other agencies

Exercise

Looking at the list above, consider what types of power you already have. Is there any way you can make even more effective use of that power? Is there an area where you currently feel lack of power? If so, what can you do to increase your power balance?

Personalities and negotiation

Each person in a negotiation brings their own personality to bear. This includes issues such as:

- life history
- recent experiences

- motivation
- age
- ethnicity
- gender
- religion
- cultural norms
- fear
- confidence levels
- experience of you
- feelings about your department

Personality brings with it **negotiating style** – a stance from which people (often instinctively) operate. In a sense we all bring to the negotiating table a set of beliefs and expectations about the process and other people involved. If we are accurate this can be very helpful and guide our conversations, but we are hampered by fear or prejudice we are unlikely to perform effectively.

A skilled negotiator will know when to use which style for best effect, and will realise that the whole of a conversation does not have to be carried out in one style.

Negotiating styles

Conflicting

Some people's negotiating style is *conflicting*, often resulting in a *win–lose* negotiation. People with this attitude are likely to disregard the needs of others and believe that their needs/values/beliefs are more important than yours. They will do what they can to defeat you by whatever means are necessary (i.e. manipulate, undermine, threaten you). This style is likely to damage any future negotiations.

Collaborative

This is a *win–win* style where the partners in the negotiation start from the belief that both are willing to negotiate. Obviously both sides will not go away with exactly what they want, but the aim is that they should go away equally happy, that neither feels defeated by the other. This approach is one that is best suited to long-term future relationships.

Compromising

With this type of negotiation people decide to, for example, split the difference 50/50. This can produce a quick result, but it can often leave the players with a niggling discomfort – 'If they gave in that easily perhaps I should have pushed for more.'

Bargaining

With a bargaining style, each party has areas of give and take – each makes and takes concessions. If you decide to use this style, take into account the following four points:

- Don't indicate that you can be easily moved from your present position.
- Move slowly, and make the other party work for each concession.
- Try to get the other person to put down 'openers' first for each concession.
- Try to get a return for every concession you make.

Coercive

This is when one person believes they can negotiate by threat, subtle or otherwise – 'If you don't do duty for me this Wednesday, I'll have to think again about helping you with that case.' This is not truly a negotiating style at all, because negotiation is about reaching an equitable agreement, not one side bullying the other. This style is likely to damage future relationships, and you should consider the consequences before you use it. Also, be prepared to have your bluff called.

Emotional

Emotion is a powerful tool, and many negotiators consider what would most sway the other party's emotions. Consider using this if you think that a passionate appeal will be more likely to succeed than cool reason. Keep in control of your own emotions during this type of negotiation; remember to be congruent in what you say, how you say it and your body language.

Logical reasoning

It is difficult to disagree with a well-constructed argument, although you may choose to combine this with an emotional approach if this seems your best bet.

Gender and negotiating

Women and men sometimes have different communication styles. Neither of these communication styles is better or worse than the other, but they can lead to differing expectations during discussion. For example, women tend to put ideas much more tentatively – 'I wonder if ...', 'Perhaps ...', 'I think ...' (when they actually know). Another approach women take is to ask questions about things they already know, to include the other person in the conversation – 'Do you think ...?', 'How would it be if ...?'

Men, on the other hand, are more likely to simply make a statement – 'The facts of the matter are ...', 'On twenty-seven occasions ...' This can lead to the man thinking the woman is indecisive and therefore easy to browbeat in a negotiation. It can also lead the woman to feel the man is overbearing and uncooperative.

Another point is that if you are negotiating as part of a meeting, women's views are much more likely to be ignored by both women and men. Often a woman will put forward an idea which is ignored; later a man will suggest the same thing and everyone acts on it as if they had never heard it before.

Of course, these are stereotypes so don't expect everyone to perform in the same way simply because of their gender. Many won't. If you are particularly interested in gender differences in conversation Deborah Tannon's books on the subject, *You Just Don't Understand* (1990) and *Talking 9 to 5* (1996), are very readable.

Cultural differences and negotiating

Cultural differences are enormously important in negotiating. For example, in Britain it is not normal to negotiate for the price of goods you buy in a shop but in some Middle Eastern countries it would be considered an insult not to do so. This makes it important that you try to learn something about your opponent's background and expectations if at all possible.

An additional point to bear in mind is that of body language. As Chapter 3 points out, there is very little that is universal in non-verbal communication – most gestures and facial expressions are different from one culture to another. Again, do your homework if appropriate to ensure that misunderstandings don't lead to unnecessary friction.

Finding common ground – 'chunking up and down'

Sometimes negotiations get stuck because agreement can't be reached about a small detail or a particular issue. If this happens, try 'chunking up'.

Negotiations can take place on several different levels, and if you get stuck at any level, try going a chunk 'higher' (to a higher number in the list below) until some common ground can be found. The levels are:

1 **Environment** – the physical context of the negotiation
2 **Specific behaviour** – what the person actually says and does in the negotiation
3 **Capabilities** – what each of you is capable of doing (e.g. you may not have the authority to make certain concessions)
4 **Beliefs** – yours and their belief systems about all aspects of the negotiation, including negotiating style
5 **Identity** – who the person is, their position in the negotiating process

Let's look at a typical social work example. Suppose you are a social worker trying to get a permanent residential place for a client, Mr Jones. For the sake of this example we'll assume that you can negotiate direct with the head of the home. When you start talking to her you say you urgently need the next available place (specific behaviour). She tells you that she has three other urgent requests lined up (specific behaviour). If this line of discussion gets nowhere you could 'chunk up' to beliefs: 'Can we agree that we both want the best for Mr Jones?' This temporarily focuses away from areas of disagreement and starts again where you can agree. By doing this, you can get back on an even keel to explore further options.

Creating alternatives

By looking at these different logical levels in negotiation you begin to create alternative approaches – an essential skill in any negotiation. Some other tips for creating alternatives are:

● First give the message you think the other side will be happy to hear.
● Begin with relatively easy to agree matters.
● Emphasise the need for agreement.
● Let the other side know that you understand their viewpoint by presenting both sides of the argument.
● Keep calm, open and flexible in your approach.
● Summarise any agreements as you go on, and see how these can lead to other options.

Confidence in negotiation

Your chances of winning any negotiation will be much less if you lack confidence. Others will see that they can bulldoze you into agreeing to their terms. Preparation and confidence in your knowledge, skills, information and power base can all help you to feel confident in negotiation. Commitment to do the best for your client will often be a major motivating force to do well. But remember that you are also important and you should fight for yourself as much as you fight for your client – something some social workers find difficult. Being assertive is about respecting yourself and others equally.

The 'Three Yes Questions' technique

If you think that you are going to have a tough time getting the other person to negotiate fairly and listen to your point of view, use the 'Three Yes Questions' technique. The idea is to find three statements they simply must agree with; these then lead you on to the big question, which is more difficult to dispute because of the discussion you've just had.

Case study – Mandy

Jim, a social worker working with disabled adults, had found a place for Mandy, aged 22, at a residential unit where she could live happily with other adults and be encouraged to develop her full potential. Mandy's mother, Ann, was reluctant to let her go. She loved Mandy and believed that no one could look after her as well as she did. The result was that Mandy was rather 'babied' and didn't do as much for herself as she could. She also had little social life outside the day centre she attended. Legally, Mandy could make up her own mind about moving, but Jim knew that she'd be unlikely to do so against her mother's wishes. Jim planned his 'Three Yes Questions' to Mandy's mother:

1   'Ann, as you know I've been looking at residential establishments for Mandy as she requested. I know this is a difficult issue for you but I wonder if we could go over a few points? Now that Mandy is 22, would you agree that she should have more of a social life?'
2   'Do you believe that at her age Mandy should be able to make her own decisions when all possible information is available?'
3   'Do you agree that Mandy will need someone to look after her when you are too old to do so?'

Once Mandy's mother had answered 'Yes' to all three questions it was much easier for Jim to get Ann to agree to the next question, 'So will you agree to Mandy moving there?'

Achieving a win–win outcome

Case study – Tom

Judy had a really tricky situation. Back from a week's leave, she found that her boss had neglected to deal with several pressing issues that had arisen in one of her cases. The client, a 13-year-old mentally ill young man, Tom, was being discharged from the Young People's Psychiatric Unit next day on the psychiatrist's instructions. It was clear to Judy that Tom was still a very sick young man. His mother was refusing to allow him home and there were no placements available in the county. She was faced with three possible negotiation tactics:

- try to persuade Tom's mother to allow him to return home
- try to persuade the psychiatrist to keep Tom in longer – at least until alternative accommodation could be found
- find alternative accommodation and then negotiate for the money to pay for it – never an easy task, especially with the current round of budget cuts

Because she was concerned that none of these possibilities might amount to anything, Judy decided to try all three alternatives.

Looking at the first possibility – returning Tom home to his mother – Judy considered each of the key questions for negotiation listed earlier in this chapter.

The personality of the players in the game

Tom's mother, Mary, was a single parent who had had a tough time in life. She had a brisk, no-nonsense approach and entirely blamed Tom's mental instability on Tom and his father (who left home when Tom was 3). She believed Tom could be 'cured' with the right help. She rarely changed her mind once it was made up. She was embarrassed by and ashamed of her son's behaviour.

The outcome you want

In trying this negotiation, Judy had several possible outcomes:

- to return Tom home permanently
- to return Tom home until a place in a suitable establishment could be found
- to return Tom home until a suitable foster placement could be found

The outcome the other side wants

Judy knew that Mary cared about Tom, even if her parenting skills were somewhat lacking – especially her inconsistent handling of him. Mary wanted Tom 'better' and believed that a place in a psychiatric unit was best.

What you will be willing to concede

Judy felt that her best line here was to offer more support to Mary if she took Tom home. Judy would try to establish regular outpatient appointments with the Young People's Unit and would get a volunteer Family Aid Friend to support Mary several times a week.

What you will be willing to accept

Judy would be happy to accept Mary taking Tom back, temporarily if necessary.

Your bottom line

Judy realised that she had no power to force Mary into anything. In this sense her bottom line did not amount to much.

What you think they will be willing to concede

Judy was not overly hopeful, but thought it possible that with persuasion Mary might just agree to her suggestion.

What you think they will be willing to accept

Judy thought that Mary might just agree to take Tom back with extra support. She suspected that Mary might bring up the subject of money, so she decided to speak to her manager about whether any type of grant could be made.

What you think their bottom line is

Mary's bottom line was likely to be complete refusal to take Tom back, even for a short period.

Bearing all this in mind, Judy prepared for the negotiation with Mary. She would:

- discuss with her what others would think about her rejecting him (an important issue with Mary, and one where Judy can use an emotional negotiating style)
- appeal to her as a mother of a needy son (again, an emotional negotiating style)
- offer additional support and (if possible) financial help (Judy plans to use a bargaining style here, with her boss working out all the relative costs of different placements for Tom)
- emphasise that Mary was only being asked to take Tom temporarily (a logical reasoning style would be effective here)
- explain the consequences for Tom of several moves in quick succession (again, an emotional style would probably bring the best results)

She chose this as a running order because she believed it would be the one that would be most appealing to Mary. Once she had planned this negotiation she used the same negotiating format to plan the conversations with the Young People's Unit and her line manager for money for an out of county placement.

Exercise

Using the format above, plan these two negotiations using the template below. You will have to make assumptions about some aspects of the negotiation. It could be helpful here to imagine yourself dealing with people you know from experience:

Conversation with the Young People's Unit

- the personality of the players in the game

- the outcome you want

- the outcome the other side wants

- what you will be willing to concede

- what you will be willing to accept

- your bottom line

- what you think they will be willing to concede

- what you think they will be willing to accept

- what you think their bottom line is

Your plan for negotiating

Step	Negotiating style
1	
2	
3	
4	
5	
6	
7	
8	
9	
10	

Conversation with your line manager for funding for Tom

- the personality of the players in the game

- the outcome you want

- the outcome the other side wants

- what you will be willing to concede

- what you will be willing to accept

- your bottom line

- what you think they will be willing to concede

- what you think they will be willing to accept

- what you think their bottom line is

Your plan for negotiating

	Step	Negotiating style
1		
2		
3		
4		
5		
6		
7		
8		
9		
10		

Chapter summary

Negotiation is when two or more people meet to reach an equitable agreement about a topic of common interest.

Preparation is the key to successful negotiation, it includes considering:

- the personality of the players in the game
- the outcome you want
- the outcome the other side wants
- what you will be willing to concede
- what you will be willing to accept
- your bottom line
- what you think they will be willing to concede
- what you think they will be willing to accept
- what you think their bottom line is

Goal setting is essential – unless you are clear exactly why you are negotiating you are unlikely to reach an unsatisfactory outcome. Goals should be well written to include outcomes which are SMART:

- Sensible
- Measurable
- Achievable
- Realistic
- Time-bound

A win–win (collaborative) approach is the most helpful in negotiation. Other styles sometimes used include emotion, logical reasoning, coercion, bargaining, conflict and compromise.

Gender and cultural differences should be considered in negotiating. Take into account the communication style of the person with whom you are dealing, both verbally and non-verbally.

Create alternative approaches so that you don't back yourself or the other party into a corner.

The 'Three Yes Questions' technique is useful where you think the other side will find little common agreement.

13 Handling passivity in others

Passivity comes in two major forms. The first is the 'normal' type of passivity where the person is very lacking in self-confidence and hesitates to make their wishes known or to risk antagonising people in any way. Their goal is to avoid conflict at all costs. They do not seek or expect to win in situations, although they may build up resentments (collect 'stamps') because their needs are not being met.

Take the example of a naturally shy child (there is some evidence that some babies are born with a predisposition to shyness, but this is not a fixed behaviour). If the parent gives appropriate encouragement the child will learn to overcome its shyness and will gradually become more outgoing. However, if the well-intentioned parent protects the shy child they are actually rewarding the shy behaviour, thus setting the pattern for later life.

Alternatively, a passive person may have learnt at some stage in their life that directly asking for what they want doesn't work. Even though they may know as adults that this is not an effective strategy, overcoming old built-in behaviour patterns may be difficult.

Passivity and power

Power is a complex issue. In a sense everyone gets power in whatever way they can. The power some people get may not be obvious to others, but it will meet *their* needs, which may be quite different from the needs of others. Passive people can often get their needs met by getting other people to 'look after them'. If you doubt this, think about a typical uncommunicative adolescent: they get a lot of attention by communicating in no more than grunts. With this type of behaviour it is difficult to be clear about whether you are actually faced with passivity or subtle aggression. Think about a child looking imploringly at a bar of chocolate without saying anything; think about an elderly lady shivering but saying nothing in the hope that you'll turn up the heating – this type of passivity is manipulative, although the person may not be consciously aware that they are acting in a manipulative way.

Passivity can arouse aggression in others

Ironically, passive people can actually find themselves faced with the very response from others they seek to avoid. People often get irritable with them because they feel frustrated at the lack of clear communication. It's infuriating when someone won't tell you what they want, won't make a decision, won't stand up for themselves. Alternatively, people simply avoid them because it's too much trouble trying to communicate effectively.

Many social work clients exhibit passive behaviour of one type or another. Some are playing a manipulative game, others are simply too low in self-esteem to speak out. Let's look in more detail at different types of passivity (see Table 13.1).

Table 13.1   Different types of passivity (non-assertion)

Form of non-assertion	Underlying intent	Example	Possible responses
Asking for reassurance	To get you to give reassurance without having to expose their vulnerability by asking for it directly.	a 'I don't suppose you'll agree but . . .' b 'Would you mind awfully if I . . .' c 'Do you like this?'	a 'Why do you think I wouldn't agree?' b 'What would *you* like to do?' c 'Are you happy with it?'
Refusing to make a decision	To avoid making a decision. This takes away all responsibility for the decision reached. The person can't be wrong because they didn't make a decision.	a 'I don't mind which we do.' b 'I'll leave it to you.' c 'You're much better at that than me.'	a 'I feel frustrated when you won't state a preference. Which would you rather do?' b 'I would rather you made the decision.' c 'I don't agree I'm better at it, but if you feel that way how could you improve your skills?'

Continued overleaf

Form of non-assertion	Underlying intent	Example	Possible responses
Making excuses	To avoid taking responsibility for their own actions. A blame game.	a 'I'm too busy to do that.' (assuming this is not literally true) b 'I didn't realise what you meant.' c 'I can't get to school on time every day.'	a 'How can you prioritise your work so that you can do this?' b 'Perhaps in future you could repeat requests back to me so that we are both clear.' c 'What would have to happen for you to get to school on time every day?'
Blaming others	The ultimate blame game. To avoid taking responsibility for their feelings or actions.	a 'He makes me angry.' b 'It's my mother's fault that I'm so bad with money.' c 'It's his fault I'm late.'	a 'How do you make yourself angry when he does that?' b 'How do you allow your mother's behaviour to make you bad with money?' c 'How have you allowed his behaviour to make you late?'
Tentatively expressing doubts	Not feeling confident enough to directly say there is a problem. Looking for help.	a 'I'm not sure...' b 'Well, I suppose...' c 'My husband's not sure about that.'	a and b 'What problems do you think that will give you?' c 'And what do you think?'
Helplessness	Refusing to take action to improve their skill level. Another version of the blame game.	a 'I'm just hopeless at maths.' b 'I can't do anything with him, he's too naughty.'	a 'What steps could you take to improve your maths?' b 'What do you believe children need in order to stop behaving badly?'

Continued overleaf

Form of non-assertion	Underlying intent	Example	Possible responses
Putting themselves down	May show poor self-esteem or may be trying to elicit condemnation.	a 'I'm so stupid.' b 'I always get everything wrong.' c 'I'm hopeless at budgeting.'	a 'What do you do to yourself that leaves you feeling stupid?' b 'Can you think of a time when you got anything right?' c 'What skills would you need to be better at budgeting?'
Being over-helpful	Trying to get approval by being helpful. May be into 'being strong' and taking on too much. May be trying to get you to feel guilty or in their debt.	a 'Let me give you a lift, I don't mind being late for dinner.' b 'I'll give Mr Jones a bath, don't worry.' c 'Yes, of course I'll swap duty with you again.'	a 'I don't want to make you late for dinner. Is there a way round this?' b 'Let's see what else you have to do this morning.' c 'I need to be sure that this won't inconvenience you too much. Shall we check our diaries?'
Unconvincing agreement (when you don't believe they actually do agree)	To avoid the conflict of saying they disagree with you.	a 'Yes, I'll make sure I always ask Mrs Robinson what she wants before I feed her.' b 'You could be right.' c 'OK, if you say so.'	a 'Even though you're saying you agree with me, I'm not sure that's what you really feel.' b 'You sound hesitant. What's worrying you?' c 'What problems might doing that give you?'

Empowering passive people

Dealing with passive people takes patience, a refusal to get caught up in their game and an ability not to get caught in the compassion trap. If you constantly help passive people they will never develop the range of skills they need to deal with life. It is worth considering that whilst people may be passive because of situations earlier in their life, whatever the reason, they lack the *skills* to act more effectively.

Take the situation of a child who was never given a choice, whose parents never said, 'Do you want to wear the red jumper or the blue jumper today?' or 'Would you like toast or cornflakes for breakfast?' How can that child learn the skill of choosing? Or the situation of a child growing up in a household where disagreement was never expressed out loud. The child will never learn the skills of disagreeing assertively and believing in his or her rights to have a viewpoint expressed. Or the child who was always told off or punished in some way for saying 'No.' This child will never learn that it has the right to refuse requests, and will fail to have the skills to do so.

Empowerment of the passive person by teaching appropriate skills (subtly if necessary) and relevant challenges is a more effective long-term approach.

Questioning skills and the passive person

You will see from the examples above that a very common way of responding to a passive person is to ask a question. There are a number of different questioning techniques which can be grouped together under four headings.

Closed questions

Closed questions are those which are easily answered with 'Yes' or 'No' or a simple fact. These are very useful for verifying information. Some examples of closed questions are:

- 'How old are you?'
- 'Did you receive the girocheque?'
- 'Did you take Jenny to the GP today?'

Open questions

Open questions are particularly useful with passive people because they are difficult to answer with a simple 'Yes' or 'No.' They often start with 'Who...?', 'When...?', 'How...?', 'What...?', 'Where...?' Examples of open questions are:

- 'What happened to make you late for the appointment?'
- 'How do you feel about that?'
- 'Who stopped you getting to the clinic on time?'
- 'Where do you intend to try next?'
- 'When do you think you will be able to do that?'

Another useful start to an open question can be 'Why ... ?', although this one should be used with care because it can sound accusing:

- 'Why did you do that?'

Follow-on questions

Follow-on questions, as the name suggests, follow on from another question to seek more information. Follow-on questions can be either open or closed depending on whether you want to clarify a point or encourage the person to expand on what they are saying. Examples of follow-on questions are:

- 'What happened then ... ?'
- 'Tell me more about that.'
- 'Why do you think that happened?'

Leading questions

Leading questions are those which suggest to the listener the answer the questioner wants. Examples of leading questions are:

- 'Didn't you realise that would happen?'
- 'You have done something about that, haven't you?'
- 'You do know how that'll make your son feel, don't you?'

Leading questions are very rarely helpful and it is wise to avoid using them altogether.

Silence – a major communication skill

A major skill to be combined with the questioning techniques is that of zipping your mouth – ask your question and shut up! It is a completely natural reaction to want to fill a silence; if you can train yourself to maintain the silence the odds are that the client will say something themselves. (Adolescents are often an exception here – they can out-silence anyone.)

Giving choosing time

Sometimes a client can be encouraged to make a choice by being given time and a choice of how to say what they want. Suppose, for example, you had to ask an elderly person if they would like to attend a day centre and received either no answer or an unconvincing one. After explaining all the pros and cons you could suggest that the client take a day or two to think through the issue, and if necessary suggest they drop you a note giving their decision. Sometimes people find it easier to write down what they consider difficult messages.

Rapport and the passive person

Establishing rapport with the passive person is essential if we are to encourage them to develop and speak out. As we have seen in Chapter 4, this can be done by matching the person in their:

- **body language** – by sitting or standing in similar ways
- **voice** – by using a similar tone, speed and pitch
- **language** – by using words and sentences of similar length
- **categories** – by talking about the types of things the passive person identifies with, if necessary using these as a way in to more 'delicate' areas
- **representational systems** – by noticing whether the person is predominantly visual, aural, feeling or logical, and selecting language to match

Generally it is recommended that we have good eye contact with the person we wish to communicate with. Sometimes with passive clients an alternative strategy is more effective. Have you ever noticed how the most deep and meaningful conversations often take place in the kitchen or the car? This can be because the people are *not* looking at each other, and for some people this makes saying difficult things much easier. Many social workers learn to use car trips for this purpose.

Chapter summary

People are passive because they either lack confidence or are 'playing a game' in some way which is manipulative.

Passive people who lack confidence often go to considerable lengths to avoid conflict – sadly, their behaviour often brings exactly the type of response they want to avoid.

Passive behaviour comes in several forms. Some examples are:

- asking for reassurance
- refusing to make a decision
- making excuses
- helplessness
- putting yourself down
- blaming others

- tentatively expressing doubt
- being overhelpful
- agreeing unconvincingly

When people use these approaches, **keep calm and respond assertively.** Often it helps to respond with a question.

There are four main types of question:

- **Open questions** which are difficult to answer with a simple 'Yes' or 'No.' These often start with 'Who...?', 'When...?', 'What...?', 'Where...?' or 'How...?' Open questions are useful for encouraging the passive person to continue speaking and providing more information.
- **Closed questions** are easy to answer with a simple fact or 'Yes' or 'No.' They are useful for verifying facts.
- **Follow-on questions** are useful for gaining more information about a topic already under discussion. They can be either open or closed depending on whether you want to encourage the person to say more or verify a fact.
- **Leading questions** suggest to the listener the answer you expect. They should be avoided if at all possible.

Silence following a question is very powerful – the passive person will usually fill the void.

Skilful rapport helps the passive person to speak out – this can be established by matching body language, voice, verbal language, categories and representational systems.

Sometimes allowing time to choose and alternative ways of telling you their choice enables the client to feel confident enough to express their wishes.

Sometimes giving the passive client an opportunity to avoid eye contact helps them to speak – sitting in a car or being involved in something active where you can naturally be looking at other things can provide just such an opportunity.

14 Keeping calm and confidence-building

Being assertive means that you're in control of yourself in any situation. Feeling in control, leaving every situation thinking 'I've handled that really well' is wonderful for your self-esteem – no more kicking yourself because you chickened out of dealing with a tough conversation; no more guilt overload because you lost your temper; no more niggling discomfort because you've put off doing something yet again.

And it's a two-way thing. When you use assertive techniques and handle a situation well, you feel better about yourself and your self-confidence increases. And by being more self-confident you are more likely to handle situations effectively. It follows therefore that as well as using the many assertive techniques detailed in this book, if you work on your self-esteem you'll increase your chances of acting assertively.

Chapter 2 looked at some of the blocks to assertion and how to deal with them. Now we'll look at some more confidence-building exercises to further develop a positive self-image.

Exercise: The price of not being assertive

Not being assertive has a cost. Costs are usually uncomfortable feelings such as guilt, worry, anger, sadness and depression. Think back over the past few weeks. What effect has any lack of assertion had on (a) your life, (b) your feelings? If it sometimes feels easy to slip back into old behaviour patterns, remember that the cost of not being assertive is almost certainly higher than the cost of learning new skills.

Exercise: Learning from a role model

One way to increase your self-confidence is to model yourself on someone you admire. Try this step by step approach to becoming more like your role model.

1   Identify someone who has skills and personal qualities you would like for yourself.
2   Select six of those skills and qualities.
3   Prioritise them in terms of which you most want.
4   Work out a plan for achieving this goal – remember to use the SMART method of writing effective goals to ensure clarity of action.
5   Tell people you trust what you plan to do so that you feel more committed and get appropriate support.
6   Remember to reward yourself when you reach each goal.
7   When you have worked on one goal successfully, move on to the next.

Case study – Jemma

Jemma had just got her first job as a probation officer. At 23 she was the youngest person in the office and felt very unsure of herself and her abilities. She didn't find her line manager an easy person but quickly realised that she admired Fran, one of the other probation officers in the team.

Jemma spent some time analysing her skills and skill gaps. She realised that her interpersonal skills were generally quite good, but she lacked confidence in saying 'No' to people, in speaking out in team meetings, in report writing and dealing with aggressive clients. Fran seemed able to do all of these things easily.

Jemma prioritised her needs. Based on her workload she decided:

1   Saying 'No' was top priority because even with the 'easy' caseload she had been given as a new worker it was clear that she was going to have to use this skill frequently.
2   Dealing with aggressive clients came next. She was already being asked to do home visits to clients whose background was largely unknown.
3   Speaking out in team meetings seemed the next step. Jemma realised that people who remain quiet are rarely noticed and certainly unlikely to get promotion. Jemma planned to go places with her job, and even though it was early days, she decided to keep this in mind at all times – an opportunity to display a professional and confident approach was never missed.

4   Report writing could wait till last, although Jemma realised that she could almost certainly develop this skill while working on the others.

Working on **saying 'No'**, Jemma asked Fran how she managed to appear so confident about doing this. Fran explained that being indirect never helped the client (or colleagues); by being straightforward and assertive everyone knew where they were. Yes, she agreed, sometimes she felt bad when the client desperately needed money or other resources, but if she couldn't do it, she couldn't and no amount of talking around the subject would change that. Jemma asked her to do some informal role plays and this greatly improved her skill.

Dealing with aggressive clients was a more difficult area simply because no one could anticipate when a client would become aggressive and so there was little chance to observe someone else in action. Jemma's line manager agreed to her going on a two-day course on the subject, and this, coupled with discussions she had with Fran and others in her team, left her feeling as prepared as she could be.

Speaking out in team meetings – Jemma noticed that Fran had a knack of saying things briefly and succinctly in team meetings, always timing her contributions just right. Because she was so new in the job, Jemma was often lost in discussions – she simply didn't know enough yet to contribute. She decided to do some homework and set herself some goals.

She studied the agenda for each meeting in advance and identified those topics she knew something about. For the others she asked her line manager to either briefly give her the background or tell her what she could read to be up to date. Armed with this knowledge she set herself the goal of saying two things in each of the next three team meetings, first working out what she could usefully add to the discussion. Then she would say three things in each of the next four team meetings, and four in each of the next four. She felt that by that time she would probably feel confident enough to speak freely.

This still left her unsure as to how to time her contributions. She asked Fran for advice. Fran suggested she write on cards key words to prompt her about what she wanted to say. Then, listening carefully to the discussion and watching body language for a suitable opening in the conversation, she could have her say. In fact she discussed with Fran before each meeting the points she wanted to make, and whenever possible Fran made an opening for her to speak.

To meet her **report writing** goal, Jemma asked her line manager to give her copies of reports he thought well written. She studied these and made a note of the general layout and how various aspects of the content were written. This led her to developing her own guidelines which, coupled with the department's official guidelines, gave her a comprehensive set of skills in this area.

Exercise: My personal and professional strengths

Ask most people to write a list of their failings and they'll do so in double quick time. Ask them to write down their strengths and it's often a different story – people are often brought up not to boast. But identifying your personal and professional strengths is as essential as working out how to improve on poor skills. You need to recognise these strengths not just for your own self-esteem but for appraisal interviews and job applications.

Write a list of your own personal and professional strengths. If you really struggle with this, ask people you trust to help – they will undoubtedly be able to see you more clearly than you see yourself.

Exercise: Stream of consciousness

We all talk to ourselves: it's a natural part of our intelligence. However, it's true to say that some of us have positive inner dialogues whilst others hear much less helpful messages. Chapter 2 gives more detail of where these messages come from, and it may be helpful to read or re-read that chapter before you do this exercise.

1   For five minutes write down as quickly as possible every random thought that comes into your head.
2   Now analyse it. Is your inner dialogue mostly positive or negative? Are you simply thinking through issues with the background assumption that you can deal with them, or are you saying to yourself, 'That'll be really difficult, I can't do that,' or 'I'll never be any good at that'? Watch out particularly for those old parent messages involving words such as 'ought', 'should', 'must', 'mustn't', 'everyone', 'no one', etc.
3   If you find you have a lot of negative messages, try to work out where they come from and work out ways to stop these thoughts in their tracks. Learn to change the way you think. 'That'll be really difficult, I can't do that' becomes 'That will probably be difficult but with the proper preparation I can make a reasonable job of it.' 'I'll never be any good at that' becomes 'I'll get better at that with practice' or 'I don't yet have those skills.'

Remember – if you're not in control of your mind, who is?

Exercise: Improving self-esteem

Many social workers would like to improve their self-esteem. Stated baldly, it is a big goal – how will you know when you've got there? By following the steps below you can work towards the 'you' you want to be:

- **Step 1** – Identify a behaviour you want to change.
- **Step 2** – Keep a record of when, where, how and why the behaviour occurs.
- **Step 3** – Work out how you can change the behaviour.
- **Step 4** – Consciously behave differently until the new behaviour has been repeated approximately 20–30 times.
- **Step 5** – Review – has the new behaviour become automatic? If not, repeat step 4 as necessary.

Behaviour change is difficult: you may need help to identify different ways of acting. It helps if you keep your goal small. Don't give yourself huge goals such as 'I'm going to be more assertive' – you will feel overwhelmed and won't know when you've reached your target. Break big goals down into manageable chunks: 'In future I will say "No" to extra work when I know I'm so busy I won't do it well' or 'In future I will ask for emotional support when I need it' or 'I will increase my ability to speak out in meetings by careful preparation. For the next two staff meetings I will say one thing, for the next two meetings I will say two things and gradually increase my contributions' or 'I will ask a trusted colleague to help me reach my goals.'

Exercise: Future fantasy

Find a quiet place and sit comfortably for a few minutes. Project your mind a year into the future and imagine yourself in a range of situations handling your-self assertively. Keep altering the picture until you feel completely happy with your future self. Go into the experience as fully as possible, seeing, hearing and feeling all aspects of your future fantasy. When you have finished, make notes on what you saw to encourage you to continue.

Keeping calm

Naturally, keeping calm is an important skill in developing assertion. It is difficult to look and feel assertive if you are so nervous that you stutter, blush, shake or simply chicken out of tackling a situation altogether. Fortunately, you can work on techniques to keep calm just as you can work on any other technique. Try to regard keeping calm as simply another skill to be learned – that's all it is.

First of all, try to identify your very first sign of feeling nervous or angry. Some people say they get butterflies in the stomach, some feel their shoulders tensing, some feel a blush beginning or notice their hands shake. Try to work out the very first sign, because by doing so you can take action at this earliest stage and stop your nervous reaction before it distracts you from handling something as well as you'd like.

Many people find that when they are getting nervous they have some negative inner dialogue running: 'I can't handle this!', 'She'll think I'm a fool', 'I mustn't say anything, because he's the boss' or whatever. If this is true for you, catch those unhelpful thoughts as they begin to intrude and replace them with positive thoughts, for example: 'I have the skills to handle this!' or 'I have the right to say what I think.'

It may be that you also have an unhelpful mental picture at stressful times, perhaps of an associated unpleasant event in the past or of yourself failing in some way. What follows is a technique for replacing these undesirable pictures and words with a positive frame of mind.

Anchoring technique

In everyday life our behaviour is 'anchored' to many signs and symbols. We are anchored to red traffic lights – we tend to stop every time. We are anchored to a baby smiling – we tend to smile back. We are anchored to people – some make us feel good, some don't.

Much of our anchoring goes back a long way. For example, do you find that a certain piece of music takes you right back to your first romance and suddenly you feel as you felt then? Or do you see someone who looks like a once loved person and feel sadness?

Smells can be as evocative as music. You smell jasmine and are immediately back on a Mediterranean holiday, walking down the road on a warm evening. You smell home-made bread and are immediately back in the bakery down the road from your childhood home.

In extreme cases these links (anchors) can be set up very quickly, and some of these can become phobias. For example, you feel sick one day in the supermarket and faint; thereafter you don't want to go into supermarkets. Luckily

these really negative and powerful connections happen relatively infrequently.

From these examples you will see that some of the anchors occurred naturally. You never intended that you would link the smell with the place or the music with the person – it just happened. On the other hand, you had to learn some of the other anchors – all the signs in the *Highway Code* for example. So you have seen that you can deliberately anchor yourself and your behaviour in desirable ways.

Below is an exercise which will enable you to set up positive and deliberate anchors to use in stressful situations. Some people find that just one repeat of the steps below is enough to set up the anchor, others have to practise up to a dozen times until it becomes established.

The aim is to set up one or more deliberate anchors to elicit a desirable mental state. As we have seen, anchors can be visual, auditory, or use a sense of smell or indeed touch. To ensure that you have as many chances as possible of establishing a strong anchor, the exercise below calls on you to use visual, auditory and touch anchors to elicit your desired state. If you are one of the few lucky people who can also conjure up a sense of smell, do add that to your anchors.

Exercise: Establishing a positive mental state

1   Think of a situation in which you would like to feel more positive.
2   Identify the positive mental state (inner resources) you would like to have in this type of situation (calm, confident – whatever would help you).
3   Now think of a time when you had those positive inner resources. It doesn't have to be a similar situation to that in step 1, it could be something completely unrelated. The important thing is that the feelings were there and were strong.
4   Now let's identify your anchors. First think of a visual mental image which you can connect with your positive inner state. It can be anything you like. If you're stuck for an image, some people find visualising a beautiful piece of scenery with calm water a useful one. You may like to use the image of the actual situation when you experienced the positive state. Second, identify a sound you can connect with that positive inner state. Again it can be anything – perhaps a sound connected with the image or a snatch of music or you saying something positive to yourself. Next, identify a touch. This should be unobtrusive and a touch that doesn't happen every day. Some people like to discreetly touch their thumb and little finger, or put one hand on their other wrist and gently press it with the middle finger.
5   Now take some time to mentally go into the situation you identified in step 3. Allow yourself to relive the experience as fully as possible. See what you

saw, hear what you heard and, most importantly, feel the positive feelings associated with the situation.

6   When the image and the feelings are really strong, use your anchors – touch whatever you've decided to touch, see whatever you've decided to see and hear whatever you've decided to hear.

7   With step 6 above you have begun to make the connections between your anchors and the positive inner state. Practise these until you feel confident that you can reproduce them at will.

When next you are in a stressful situation, you simply use your anchors and your positive inner state will click in to calm you down.

Distracting yourself from stress

Most people find that anchoring is a very powerful tool to ensure positive inner states in stressful situations. Other people find it is enough to simply use deep breathing. At the first sign of nervousness or anger setting in, consciously begin to breathe deeply, but don't take too many really deep breaths or you'll pass out – not more than four or five. Deep breathing has two advantages. First, just thinking about your breathing will distract you briefly from the approaching stress symptoms and thus stop any automatic panic reactions. Second, it will overcome the tendency to hyperventilate, thus ensuring that you get enough oxygen to your brain to deal effectively with the situation.

Using visualisation to keep calm

There are many visualisations which aid calmness. Try this one if you have a particularly difficult person in your life.

Get a mental image of that person. Now put Mickey Mouse ears on them, and paint their face like a clown. Next, give them a revolving spotted bow tie, and a baggy, brightly coloured T-shirt tucked into cycle shorts. Finally add odd socks and shoes. If your mental image is big (as it often is with difficult people), shrink it down until the person is only a few centimetres high.

If you think this mental image will make you laugh at a crucial moment, instead of making the person look ridiculous, fade the mental image of them until they are ghostlike and shrink them down.

This fading and shrinking of unwanted mental images is very effective. Perhaps in difficult moments you get a flashback from an earlier time. Shrink and fade that picture. Put a frame round it and turn it into a photo which you place on a far distant mental wall. It's there for reference when you need it, but no longer has a huge impact. If you do this several times you will begin to change the way the image appears and the impact it has.

Catastrophising the event

Sometimes our fantasies about a situation make us feel nervous, when the reality is something much less threatening. As well as asking yourself, 'What's the worst that can happen?' (often surprisingly little!) it can help to catastrophise the situation in your mind before you tackle it. Ask yourself, 'If I do it, will I die? Will I be maimed? Will the person shoot me? Will I lose my job?' By doing this type of thinking you realise that very little that is really bad is likely to happen, and you approach the situation with more confidence and calmness.

Action plan

In the questionnaire below, make notes about any changes you would like to make towards being more assertive. Remember to make your early goals easy to achieve to encourage you to continue.

Goal 1 What might help? What might hinder?
Goal 2 What might help? What might hinder?

Goal 3

What might help?

What might hinder?

Goal 4

What might help?

What might hinder?

Chapter summary

A deep inner sense of confidence and calmness is the very best aid to assertiveness – if at times either seems out of reach, remember that they are both achievable goals.

'Confidence' is a rather vague term – it's difficult to define and difficult to know when you've achieved it. However, it can be achieved by identifying the areas in which you'd like more confidence, and then tackling one or more until you are happy with them before moving on to another. In this way you can become more confident at speaking out in meetings, saying 'No,' making your opinion heard, believing in yourself or any other goal you decide.

You can increase your confidence by:

- learning from a role model
- considering the cost of not being assertive
- identifying your strengths
- becoming aware of your stream of consciousness and working on negative thinking patterns
- developing a future fantasy of yourself as an assertive person

Calmness can also be developed step by step. It is a skill you undoubtedly already possess or you would certainly not be doing the job you now do. You can develop the skill of calmness by:

- identifying your first stress signal and acting on it
- using the anchoring technique
- using a calming visualisation
- catastrophising the event
- establishing a positive mental state

Postscript

I hope that you have found/will find the techniques and advice in this book useful. I have been teaching assertiveness training for more than ten years to social workers, managers, schoolchildren, unemployed people, workers – in fact a wide variety of people. It has been a source of joy to see people gain insight into their own behaviour and that of others, to see them gain skills and confidence to face their future. Some take off like a rocket almost as if my giving them permission to be a different person was all they needed. Most, like me when I first learned these skills in 1981, learn the skills gradually, practise them, and increasingly gain confidence and competence.

Being assertive is a pleasure, freeing us from old unhelpful patterns and moving us forward to be the person we want to be. All you have to lose is your fear!

Let me leave you with an inspiring quote from a course evaluation form:

I have changed from being a 'Could I?' person to an 'I can!' person.

You can too ...

Bibliography

Asbell, B. & Wynn, K. (1992) *Look Yourself Up*, London: Fourth Estate

Back, K. & Back, K. (1982) *Assertiveness at Work*, London: McGraw-Hill

Berne, E. (1979) *Games People Play*, London: Penguin

Bibby, Pauline (1994) *Personal Safety for Social Workers*, Aldershot: Arena

Brady, Eric (1993) *Coping with Violent Behaviour*, Harlow: Longman

Charvet, S.R. (1995) *Words that Change Minds*, Carmarthen: Kendall/Hunt

Cox, G. & Dainow, D. (1987) *Making the Most of Yourself*, London: Sheldon Press

Dickson, A. (1982) *The Right to be You*, London: Quartet

Dixon, P. (1993) *Making the Difference,* Oxford: Heinemann

Dyer, W.W. (1990) *Pulling Your Own Strings*, London: Arrow Books

Fritchie, Rennie *Working with Assertiveness*, BBC Training Videos

Glass, Lillian (1992) *He Says, She Says*, London: Piatkus

Glass, Lillian (1993) *Confident Conversation*, London: Piatkus

Gray, John (1993) *Men are from Mars, Women are from Venus*, London: Thorsons

Haden, Elgin S. (1993) *Genderspeak*, New York: Wiley

Hambly, K. (1987) *How to Improve Your Confidence*, London: Sheldon Press

Harris, T. (1976) *I'm OK, You're OK*, London: Avon

Hawkes-Whiteheam, C. (1995) *Assertiveness: A Quick Guide*, Cambridge: Daniels

Horn, S. (1996) *Tongue Fu!*, New York: St Martin's Griffin

Laborde, Genie Z. (1994) *Influencing with Integrity*, Palo Alto, California: Syntony Publishing

Lindefield, G. (1989) *Super Confidence*, London: Thorsons

Lyle, Jane (1990) *Body Language*, London: Reed

More, Willie (1993) *The A-B-C of Handling Aggression*, Birmingham: Pepar

O'Connor, J. & Seymour, J. (1993) *Introducing NLP*, London: Aquarian Press

Paul, Nancy (1985) *The Right to be You*, Bromley: Chartwell-Bratt

Pearson, Vida (1992) *The Causes of Aggression*, Sheffield: Hallam University

Pease, Allan (1988) *Body Language*, London: Sheldon Press

Phelps, S. & Austin, N. (1975) *The Assertive Woman*, California: Impact

Powell, John (1969) *Why am I Afraid to Tell You Who I am?*, London: Fount

Proto, Louis (1989) *Who's Pulling Your Strings?*, London: Thorsons

Richardson, Jerry (1992) *The Magic of Rapport*, California: Capitola, Meta Publications

Schapiro, Nichole (1993) *Negotiating For Your Life*, New York: Henry Holt

Tannon, Deborah (1990) *You Just Don't Understand*, Carmarthen: Meta, Virago

Walther, G.R. (1993) *Say What You Mean And Get What You Want*, London: Piatkus

Wilson-Brown, Gwynne (1994) *The Assertive Teacher*, Aldershot: Arena

Index

Aggressive behaviour 5–9, 15
  assessing 2–4
Aggression, handling 125–40

Belief systems 20–22, 31–2, 33
  and values 101
  and rights 57–9, 66
  and criticism 105–7
Boundary setting 120, 124
Broken record and requests 77
  and criticising 100

Chunking 148
Compassion trap 10–11
Confrontation 134
Criticism 34
  and receiving 100
  and giving 91–100
Cultural difference 37, 38, 44, 51, 129

Digressers, dealing with 88

Ego states 23–5, 28, 105–6, 107–8
Empowerment 91
Eye movements 54

Feedback, giving 91
Fogging 133

Game playing 29–31
Gender and assertiveness 17–18, 33, 41,
  44, 51
Goal setting 47, 55, 144
Guilt 118
  overcoming 119

Home visits and safety 137–8

Indirectly aggressive behaviour 12, 16
Interruptions 87

Keeping calm 167–177

Lie detection 40

Making requests 60, 71
Making mistakes 60
Matching categories 50–51, 55
Matching language 50
Matching representational systems 52,
  55
Matching voice tone 49–50, 55
Meetings 81
  and rights 63, 65
Meta level 79
Mirroring 40, 43, 44, 47, 55
Mixed messages 91
Mood change 43

Needs, own 11
Negative enquiry 113
Negotiating 144–57
  and gender 148
  and cultural differences 148
NLP 49, 53
Non-verbal communication, 35–44, 51
  and meetings 86–7
  and aggression 131
Non-verbal leakage 35, 41, 44, 132

Opposing views, stating 87
Over-talkers, stopping 88

Pacing and leading 49
Parent messages 18, 20, 23, 33, 170

Passive behaviour 9–11, 15,
    and power 159
    and questioning skills 163
Physical threat 37
Praise, giving 100

Questioning 163–4

Rapport 45–55,
    and passive people 165
Reality 32
Refusal, consequences of 118
Rights 57–70
    and criticising 94

and management 65
and meetings 82–3

Sarcasm and put-downs 113
Saying No 60, 117–24
    advantages of 119, 124
Self-esteem 32–3, 128, 167, 171
Stamps, collecting 11–12
Support and rights 64, 71

Transactional analysis 23–31, 34

Voice, tone 133